What Are We Going to Do with All These Rotting Fish?

What Are We Going to Do with All These Rotting Fish?

and Seven Other Short Plays
for Church and Community

edited by
NORMAN HABEL

illustrations
by John Maakestad

FORTRESS PRESS ● PHILADELPHIA

Library of Congress Catalogue Card Number 76-119766

2766B70   Printed in U.S.A.   1-147

Playing with this Book

Drama opens the door to parts of ourselves or our world. Our feelings and our thoughts take on flesh. Our dreams and our fears come to life. We get involved in the conflicts and power of life without leaving our seats. We react. We shout. We cry. We hate. We love. And we risk. We risk ourselves before the people we know. We risk our future before their altar. We expose ourselves in the action of the play. And that is what we want to happen. Hence it is desirable to stage these plays as close to the audience as possible. If they are performed in a chancel, extend the chancel into the nave. Draw the congregation into the conflict of the play. If they are done in a hall, consider presenting them in the round. But never let your viewers escape the sharp point of each play. For these plays are pointed. They focus on concerns that divide youth and adults. They take a human situation and give it a dramatic form to force our response. Response is vital. And subsequent dialogue between youth and adults is encouraged. In fact, that goal was primary in the selection of these plays. They are designed to spark real confrontation between a congregation and its kids. And so they should be performed boldly with that aim in mind. Don't soften the points of the plays. Let them reach the soft spots in our souls.

What are some of those points? Sex, demonstrations, miracles, dying, human relations, Jesus Christ, Christmas, and Calvary are subjects of the plays. But the point or points of each play are much more personal and ambiguous. They catch you by surprise if you listen with faith. Why didn't the three kids go through with their demonstration in the church? Why should the three wise men be portrayed as blundering astrologers? Even these are superficial questions. In the last analysis we are concerned about the human feelings, faith, and values of the characters of the plays wherever they are trapped. For those characters have a kinship with us. Let them be seen on stage. And let them be heard by honest discussion between youth and adults after the play.

Play with these plays in any way you wish. Keep stage setting to a minimum. Suggest the scenes and highlight the characters. Let the generation gap questions be heard in your circle. This book provides a few fire crackers to wake us up to some of these questions.

The Plays in This Book

CONTENTS

What Are We Going to Do with All These Rotting Fish?

by RICHARD
URDAHL

A chancel drama of sorts based on a
rather free reading of Luke 5:1-11

Characters

SAM: Fortyish; less than polished; the best darned
fisherman on the lake; as a youth he was a
rabbinical student but he finally tired of waiting.

RUNT: Thirtyish; ever loyal; Sam's junior partner;
as a child he was much neglected.

ANGELICA: Mid-twentyish; newly married; her one
not-so-secret ambition in life is to live as an
angel.

LARS: Mid-twentyish; while holidaying in the sunny
south, he met and married Angelica; his oft
uttered hope in life is that Angelica falls.

CARPE DIEM: "Carp the Shark," as he is known to
his friends, is a first-century free enterpriser who
unerringly knows both what and whom to do.

Setting

The seashore.

The first third of the first century, that point in
history that is both dated and dateless, depending on
whether you are looking at a calendar or in a mirror.

Suggestion

Let the performance expose the rich humor of the
human in the Scriptures. The play itself can open
the door to an honest discussion of the role and
meaning of the Scriptures for "scientific" young
people.

SAM: What are we going to do with all these damn fish?

RUNT: Good question, Sam.

SAM: What are we going to do with all these damn, rotting fish?

RUNT: Good question, Sam.

SAM: What are we going to do with all these damn, rotting, stinking fish?

RUNT: Good question, Sam.

SAM: What a scene . . . what a scene! It started out as a kind'a brand-spanking-new, shiney miracle but . . . Pow! . . . it has ended as one great big, fat, slimey mess!

RUNT: Right, Sam.

SAM: The Big Man says, "Push out now into deep water and let down your nets for a catch." And simple Simon . . . old Loud Mouth Simon . . . says, "O.K., Boss!"

RUNT: Right, Sam.

SAM: And now we're stuck with two boat loads of piscatorial putrescence!

RUNT: Right, Sam.

SAM: I don't know who I'm angrier at . . . old Loud Mouth or the Big Man?

RUNT: Me neither, Sam.

SAM: I'd never ask a guy to forsake his fish and follow me!

RUNT: Me neither, Sam.

SAM: And I don't think I'd be dumb enough to do it if anyone asked me to!

RUNT: Me neither, Sam.

SAM: Fish I know. . . .

RUNT: Sure, Sam.

SAM: . . . boats I know. . . .

RUNT: Sure, Sam.

SAM: . . . and nets I know!

RUNT: Sure, Sam.

SAM: What are we going to do with all these damn fish?

RUNT: Good question, Sam.

SAM: What are we going to do with all these damn, rotting fish?

RUNT: Good question, Sam.

SAM: What are we going to do with all these damn, rotting, stinking fish?

RUNT: Good question, Sam.

SAM: Here I thought that the Big Man was giving us all the fixens for a real slam-bang fish fry!

RUNT: Sure, Sam.

SAM: When that fell through you'd of thought that at least some of the crowd would have stayed behind long enough to bury the fish!

RUNT: Sure, Sam.

SAM: Everyone knows there's a mighty quick count to the cry, "Fresh fish!" Three cries and you're out!

RUNT: Fresh fish!

SAM: Strike one!

RUNT: Fresh fish!!

SAM: Strike two!!

4

RUNT: Fresh fish!!!

SAM: You're out!!! YUCK!!!!

[ANGELICA and LARS *enter. She is filled with exuberance; he isn't.*]

ANGELICA: Did he come this way?

SAM: Who?

RUNT: Who?

ANGELICA: The Big Man, of course! We've been looking for him for days . . . weeks . . . months! Has he been here?

SAM: Yup.

RUNT: Yup.

ANGELICA: Are you sure?

SAM: Yup.

RUNT: Yup.

ANGELICA: Did you hear that, my beloved!

[*She runs to* LARS *and gives him a chaste embrace. When he responds with an incipiently besmirching embrace, she pulls away and returns to* SAM *and* RUNT.]

ANGELICA: You must pardon our impatience and incredulity. It's just that we've walked so far and are so very tired. It seems that we're always just a day late. All we have found so far are the witnesses to his wondrous presence: the beggar who saw his first sunset . . . the little granny who heard her first chirp from a Yellow Bellied Sap Sucker . . . the skinny little couple that danced their first hora . . . the Scarlet Woman now dressed in White. . . .

LARS: Black!

ANGELICA: . . . oh, we have seen his miraculous calling

5

cards lavishly scattered on village and countryside, but him, we've not seen!

SAM: Well, little lady, we've got one of his calling cards here and believe me, it's a whopper!

RUNT: Right you are, Sam.

SAM: It makes all those other miracles look like pretty small potatoes.

RUNT: Right you are, Sam.

SAM: It's not one of them two-bit miracles that you have to see in order to believe.

RUNT: Right you are, Sam.

ANGELICA: Did you hear that, my beloved?

[*She moves toward her husband; his arms are outstretched. When she remembers the last encounter, she turns quickly to* SAM.]

ANGELICA: Oh, please, sir . . . please, please! Where is this wondrous work? Just the sight of it will give us the strength to continue our search for him!

SAM: Take a deep breath, little lady, you'll find it!

ANGELICA: That's impossible! The stench from that pile of rotten fish is too great!

SAM: Don't knock the fish, honey. That's your miracle.

ANGELICA: Rotten fish? I don't understand!

SAM: I don't either, honey, but the Big Man's been here and there's the evidence . . . one of his calling cards . . . lavishly piled on the shore.

ANGELICA: You must be joking.

SAM: Would I joke about fish?

RUNT: Nosiree, Sam.

SAM: Would I joke about rotting fish?

RUNT: Nosiree, Sam.

SAM: Would I joke about rotting, stinking fish?

RUNT: Nosiree, Sam.

SAM: Would I joke about rotting, stinking fish?

RUNT: Nosiree, Sam.

ANGELICA: Were you here when it happened?

SAM: I was here.

RUNT: He was here.

ANGELICA: Did you see it happen?

SAM: I saw it.

RUNT: He saw it.

ANGELICA: Are you sure it was he?

SAM: It was him.

RUNT: It was him.

ANGELICA [*rapturously*]: Then this must be one of his mystery miracles and as such it has meaning only to the eyes of the faithful!

SAM: I suspect that it also means something to the nostrils of the unfaithful! And I'll just bet you that it speaks more powerfully to my nose than it does to your eyes!

ANGELICA: I wonder . . . oh, how I wonder what he was trying to say through these fish?

LARS: Please, dear wife, don't be presumptuous. Only the learned men sitting on alabaster benches can discern the meaning of this sign. They alone can banish our wonder. True, we can see. But then we must ask them if what we saw was what we ought to have seen or if they see that what we saw ought to have been seen as we saw it. At least, that's the way I see it.

ANGELICA: Right you are, dear husband. As the sage said: Full heart, empty head! Oh, how blessed it is that we can bring our questions to the men on the alabaster benches!

7

LARS: And how blessed it is that we can bring our money to them also. As the sage said: Without salary, the saint is silent!

SAM: I don't mean to knock another man's trade, but I don't have to have the boys resting their overstuffed brains on alabaster benches tell me what this business is all about.

RUNT: Me neither, Sam.

ANGELICA [*offended, shocked, stunned, but not speechless*]: Trade. . . . Over-stuffed brains. . . . You don't need them to tell you. . . . By the beard of the prophet, sir, you have a sour tongue!

SAM: I, ma'am, have a sour nose!

ANGELICA: Lars! Say something!

LARS: You, sir, are unlettered, unkempt, and uncouth!

SAM: Listen, buddy . . . as the sage hath said: You can just hug my nasturtiums and kiss my asters!

LARS: O.K., Mack, you asked for it! I'm going to. . . .

ANGELICA: Lars!

LARS: . . . pray for you.

SAM: Well, that's a safe thought! Lofty . . . noble . . . kind . . . but oh so safe! Tell you what, buddy, let her pray for me and then you can help us get rid of these stinking fish!

ANGELICA: Not on your life! We'll not have the purity of our spiritual pilgrimage besmirched by continued conversation with one whose ultimate concern does not reach beyond scales, gills, and dorsal fins! You got yourself into this mess . . . you can just go ahead and get yourself out of it!

SAM: I did not get myself into this mess! Have you

8

forgotten who really caught these fish? Have you forgotten that you're looking at and breathing in a miracle?

ANGELICA [*momentarily silenced by this reminder*]: Well . . . I don't believe that he caught them!

SAM: Have I ever lied to you before?

RUNT: Sam ain't never lied to anybody, anywhere at any time whatsoever and whithersoever!

SAM: Buddy!

RUNT: Friend!

[*They clasp arms and do a little dance.*]

ANGELICA: Well, then, I think that you just imagined that he caught them!

SAM: Me? Me . . . imagined that he caught them? Imagined? Listen, lady. I'm too dumb to imagine anything! I see, I hear, I taste, I touch, I smell but believe me . . . I don't imagine. My brain is so small that the softest sound . . . the faintest light . . . fills it so completely that there's not even room for gnat's nose's wart's hair let alone room for imagination!

RUNT: He ain't kiddin', ma'am!

SAM: Buddy!

RUNT: Friend!

[*They do another little two-step.* LARS *tries to join them in some sort of a circle dance.*]

ANGELICA: Lars! How disgustingly carnal!

LARS [*lustily*]: Yeh!!

ANGELICA: If you didn't imagine it . . . then . . . you must have seen some sort of vision.

SAM: Honey . . . baby . . . remember, you're talking to a poor, simple, honest clod. Woman, remember, visions are triggered by ideas! And me . . . me . . . I don't even know the difference between theology and ichthyology. No, lady, I don't imagine things and I don't see visions! But I know what I see and I believe what I see! I know what I hear and I believe what I hear!

ANGELICA [*obviously touched by this crude innocence*]: My dear fellow, I've done you a great wrong . . . a great wrong! I am so shamed! Little did I realize that your faith was so childlike! It is the kind of faith for which I am searching!

SAM: Childlike, my rosey-red umbabah! What I've been talking about has nothing whatsoever to do with a childlike faith. As a matter of fact, it's the exact opposite. Now, if you really wanna know about imagination and visions and stuff like that then talk to a kid, any kid, your own kid!

ANGELICA: We have no children, alas.

LARS: They are yet in my loins, alas!

ANGELICA: Lars! That sounded distressingly carnal!

LARS: And it looks as though that is about as close as I'm ever going to get to the real thing!

RUNT: Alas, would you like to talk about it?

ANGELICA: Talk about it? Talk about what? Just what is the issue here?

LARS: That's just it . . . there is no issue!

RUNT: Alas!

LARS [*placing his hand on* RUNT's *shoulder*]: Buddy!

RUNT [*placing his hand on* LAR's *shoulder*]: Friend!

SAM: O.K., little lady, since you're interested in a childlike faith, let me tell you about my kid. Talk about imagination. Talk about seeing things . . .

you know, like visions! Well, just yesterday she told me that she saw something that had three heads, seven feet, twelve arms, and a tail that was made out of seventy-seven gigantic olive pits!

ANGELICA: Did you hear that? Did you hear that? Three . . . seven . . . twelve . . . seventy-seven! Such symbolism! Truly the harp within her spirit was strummed by heavenly zephyrs!

SAM: Harp, hades! She had a stomachache! She'd eaten seventy-seven olives! And it seems that she only spit out seventy pits! Man, do we ever have the action at our house! Say, friend, just what kind of pots do you make?

LARS [*trying to change the subject*]: Let's get back to the fish.

SAM: With shovels?

LARS: Of course not! I want to hear your non-childlike interpretation of this miracle. Since you question the veracity of learned men and belittle those who don't, I would like to hear what these fish say to you. They surely must say something to you!

SAM: Oh, they do . . . they do! And you want to hear what they say to me?

ANGELICA: With all my heart I do?

LARS: Why not?

RUNT: Sock it to 'em, Sam!

SAM: Well, now . . . I . . . don't exactly . . . I don't know exactly where I should begin! I haven't really philosophized since . . . well . . . since last year's harvest festival at Obadiah's wine press. [*They grab hands and do a particularly wild dance.*]

11

Lars: Let's forget the Bash in the Mash for a minute and return to the question. Just what is it that these fish say to you? Remember?

Sam: Of course I do. The words . . . the words come bleedingly forth through those sharp, boney jaws . . . bleedingly, I say, they come forth . . . but they are lovingly bathed, cleansed, purified by the soft down of angel wings . . . wings that have been dipped in the azure pools of morning's dew . . . up they come . . . caught by lordly Zephyrs . . . shaped and harmonized by the celestial song writer . . . they ride through the heavenly haze on blasts from golden trumpets saying. . . .

Angelica [*nearly undone by suspense*]: Yes?

Sam: . . . saying. . . .

Angelica: Yes . . . yes?

Sam: . . . saying. . . .

Angelica: Yes, yes, yes, yes!

Sam: . . . saying. . . . Bury us cuz we stink!

[*There is shocked silence. It first appears that* Angelica *will claw* Sam; *instead, she begins to sob softly. As her sobbing becomes torrential she throws herself into* Lars' *arms.*]

Lars: There, there, my sweet. It's all right . . . everything is O.K. . . . just calm down.

Angelica: Forgive me, dear husband . . . forgive these foolish, girlish tears.

Lars: It's all right, my darling . . . tears were meant for girls and girls were meant for. . . .

Angelica: But tears are such a weak, womanly response!

Lars: Relax, pet. . . don't resist any weak, womanly

response. I have my weaknesses too! Let us find strength in each other's weaknesses. There is an inn not too far back. We can return to our pilgrimage tomorrow. Tonight let us find refreshment. . . .

ANGELICA: For our spirits?

LARS: And for our bodies! Come, now, to the inn! We couldn't possibly catch up with the Big Man today!

SAM: Wrong again, Mack. He's not more than five miles from here . . . and if you both really hoof it you could make it before sundown.

LARS [*viciously*]: Shut up!

ANGELICA [*to* SAM]: Are you sure?

SAM: Absolutely!

ANGELICA: Totally, completely, thoroughly sure?

RUNT: Absolutely!

LARS: Will you both knock it off!

ANGELICA: Oh, Lars . . . this is no time for talking about a nice quiet inn! Whatever can you be thinking about?

LARS: The wonders of creation.

ANGELICA: Oh, for goodness' sake, let the psalmists celebrate the wonders of creation. Who can think of sleeping at a time like this?

LARS: I certainly wasn't!

SAM: Come on, buddy, listen to the little woman. The big show isn't that far away! Use the boy scout pace and you'll be there before sundown!

ANGELICA: Hurry, beloved, hurry! We have tarried too long! One more word and we might just as well call it quits for today!

LARS [*pausing for a moment*]: As I was saying earlier. . . .

[*He is interrupted by the arrival of* CARPE DIEM.]

CARPE [*with slick-tongued ease*]: Good afternoon friends and neighbors, yes, indeed, a pleasant good afternoon to you all! Notice that I call you "friends," yes, indeed, "friends." Why, you ask, do I so freely, so unreservedly, so all-embracingly bestow this hallowed appellation on one and all? Why? That's a good question and it deserves a good answer! Well, friends and neighbors, I'm here to tell you that I, yours truly, Carpe Diem, have never, I repeat, have never met a man I didn't like or a woman I didn't love.

Notice also that I call you "neighbors," yes, indeed, the word is "neighbors"! Why, you ask, do. . . .

RUNT: I didn't ask.

CARPE: . . . ah, my good young friend, audibly, no, which is the hallmark of an agile mind and good breeding, and we all know, I repeat, we all know how desperately this great land of ours needs good breeding, yes sir, good breeding from top to bottom. . . . For it is written. . . . What is that godawful smell?

RUNT: Rotten fish! What'd you think it was? Radiant Rosie's Pleasure Emporium?

CARPE: What'd I tell you? Agile mind . . . agile, agile, agile! And I'm here to tell. . . .

SAM: O.K., neighbor, how can we be of assistance to you? And if you don't mind, could we get right to the point?

CARPE: Right to the point . . . right to the point!

That's what I like! A man of action! Cut through the red tape! Smash through the obstacles! Eradicate all shilly-shallying! Get right to the point. . . . I'm looking for some fishing boats!

SAM: Whose?

CARPE: Mine.

SAM: Yours?

CARPE: Yes, indeed! Just hours ago I became the proud, I repeat, proud owner of two of the finest boats on this lake, this very lake.

SAM: So who'd you buy them from?

CARPE: Who'd I buy them from . . . buy them from? I? What a commercial mentality you have, sir! I see facts and figures, profit and loss, barter and trade written all over you, sir! And that's not good, I repeat, that's not good at all. . . . Why, it's . . . it's nothing less than a portent of illness! Ominous, ominous, ominous! Let me open your eyes to a whole new world, my friend, I repeat, a whole new world, the world of grace! Yes, that's the word, grace . . . undeserved favor, unmerited gifts, unearned treasure! Friend, people gave me, I repeat, gave me these boats! Open your eyes, neighbors, to this other world . . . this new world!

RUNT: So give us something already!

CARPE: Agile, agile, agile!

SAM: Who gave you their boats?

CARPE: I'm glad you asked! Some splendid chaps, yes sirree sir, top-drawer men all, from good stock, I repeat, good stock . . . salt of the earth . . . one-of-a-kind types they are, sir, and I mean to tell you. . . .

SAM: Their names?

CARPE: Simon Peter and his partners. You know them?

SAM: Sure, I know old Loud Mouth and the Short Fuse Brothers.

CARPE: Sir, you are talking about holy men!

SAM: No I'm not, I'm only talking about my old fishing buddies.

CARPE: But these men have just left everything they own. . . . I mean I'm here to tell you that they have left . . . renounced . . . all their material possessions in order to follow the Big Man! And if that's not holiness then I don't know holiness!

ANGELICA: The Big Man?!? You've seen him?

CARPE: Not only have I seen him, my little pretty, I had lunch with him the day before yesterday!

ANGELICA [*too good to be truish*]: I don't believe you.

CARPE: Then ask . . . well, ask anybody! There must have been about five thousand of us there!

SAM: How did the boys happen to give you their boats?

CARPE: I'm glad you asked! There I was sitting in this dingy bistro when they walked in for a little something to cut the trail dust from their throats, and I'm here to tell you that they soon cut it away . . . every last particle they cut away! Anyway, I heard them talking about how great it was to be free at last . . . those were their words, the very words . . . free at last . . . from the nonessentials of life! They had left everything, I repeat, everything behind. Then they began to brag about the things they had

16

given up . . . I mean, they really went to it . . . talk about your one-up-manship, if you know what I mean! Anyway, they had left boats, nets, houses, farms, savings accounts, blue-chip stocks . . . . Man, I'm here to tell you that I took an immediate interest in renunciation! I mean, those nonessentials really grabbed me!

SAM: So what happened next?

CARPE: I asked them, I mean very politely I asked them what they planned to do with those renounced nonessentials. They said, "Nothing!" Did you hear that? The word was "Nothing!" But Peter . . . now get this . . . Peter said, "Let them rot! R-O-T . . . rot!" Oh, that man does have a way with words! "You mean that you don't want them?" I queried. And I'm here to tell you they said . . . to a man . . . they said, "No!"

SAM: So you said?

CARPE: I'm glad you asked! So I said, "That's mighty poor stewardship!" James and John thundered out a curse . . . oh, those two are rough ones, I repeat, rough ones! But Peter said . . . although it was more like a command . . . "Speak on! You have Peter's ear!". . . oh, he does put a fancy turn in a phrase!

SAM: And you spoke on?

CARPE: You'd better believe it, buddy! Very simply, very directly, and very quickly I said, "Rather than letting your property go to waste . . . for one thing, just think how that would reduce property values . . . rather than letting it go to waste, why not give it to me? I'll use it." . . . Now get this . . . "I'll use it as a sacred trust!" And what do you know, I repeat, what do you know . . . they all signed everything over to me!

SAM: Everything?

CARPE: You are so right . . . so gloriously right! And that's not all! I repeat, that's not all! They spread the word among other holy men and soon I was deluged, yes, the word is deluged, soon I was deluged with nonessentials! [*He pulls a scroll from his pocket; one end rolls down to the ground and about three feet along the ground.*] I'm here to tell you that in the last two days I've picked up twelve boats, all fully equipped, four fallow fields, one fabulously famous fig farm, a sizeable stand of sycamore trees, eleven lovely lotus pools, six-and-a half herds of gaunt goats, a crippled but quaint camel—it'll make a nice pet for a child!—four town houses, a cheese factory and . . . oh yes, one little old man, I mean he was little and he was old. . . . Obadiah was his name . . . anyway, this fellow gave me his vineyard . . . wine press included! Vive la Renunciation!!!

RUNT: Obadiah must'a been hittin' the sauce pretty hard!

SAM: So now you're getting ready to settle down here as the richest man in these parts!

CARPE: Not on your life, buster! I'm going to follow the Big Man. I mean to tell you that I'm going to follow him over hill and dale! Just think, I repeat, just think what the pickings will be like when he hits the big cities! Not only that, my friend, just think . . . just think . . . oh, it nearly drives me crazy . . . just think what will happen when the movement goes international! I'm here to tell you that the nonessentials in the gentile world are absolutely staggering, yes, the word is staggering!

SAM: But who's going to look after things while you're on the trail?

CARPE: Cousins! Would you believe it . . . by actual count, I have one hundred and thirty-eight cousins! And all of them have cousins!

ANGELICA [*eagerly*]: Are you returning to the Big Man tonight?

CARPE: Just as soon as I get the registration numbers from these boats!

ANGELICA: May we go with you?

LARS: No! I'm not moving another step!

ANGELICA: Lars? What in the world are you saying?

LARS: You heard me.

ANGELICA: But I don't understand you! Don't you realize that our search hasn't ended . . . oh, we're very close to the end . . . but it hasn't ended yet!

LARS: It has for me. I now know what I set out to learn. Any more searching would be based on a kind of indecent curiosity. Curiosity may stretch the mind but it also strangles the heart.

ANGELICA: Oh, Lars, what kind of drivel have you been reading now?

LARS: I haven't been reading . . . just thinking.

RUNT: How curious!

ANGELICA: Now, just a moment! That's enough of that! He's my husband . . . and if anyone is going to point out his inconsistencies it'll be me! But we've no time for that now. I know this will shock you . . . I'm afraid that it will even hurt you . . . but I must . . . I simply must continue the search. I am going with Mr. Carpe.

CARPE: One moment, little lady, just one little moment if you please. As one neighbor to another I'm happy . . . yes, the word was happy . . . to offer you my services; however, precedent and protocol require, I repeat, require that I ask the professional question: what do you have to renounce?

ANGELICA: A pottery!

LARS: What?

ANGELICA: A half-interest in a pottery.

LARS: Just one little minute! You've already renounced one of my businesses! You're not renouncing the other one too!

CARPE: O ye of little faith!

SAM: He is not a man of little faith! It is precisely because he is a man of faith that he refuses to get caught up in this rat race . . . this carnival!

CARPE [*feigning some sort of stroke*]: A chair . . . a chair . . . gimme a chair . . . a bench . . . a rock will do . . . water . . . please, a cup of water . . . such profanation has undone me! Rat Race???? Carnival???? What a way to talk about the Big Man! Woe is me! Water . . . please . . . water . . . or a snort of wine if you have it!

SAM: Knock it off, fella! I was not talking about the Big Man! And I was not talking about the handful of guys that he looked straight in the eye and said . . . to them . . . not to me, not to you, not to the crowd . . . but to them: "Follow me!" No, I wasn't talking about those cats! I was talking about the hundreds, and I suppose there'll soon be thousands, of faithless people . . . yes, friend, the word was "faithless" . . . I was talking about all the faithless people who go running after him, day after day, month after month, waiting, waiting, always waiting to see if he is the promised one. Hell, I know he is the promised one and you know and you know and you know! So why run through life as though we really didn't know . . . as though we were waiting for that one big deed that would finally convince us that he is the Promised One and that our daily lives are caught up in that Promise?

ANGELICA: But . . . well . . . well, it's easy for you to say that! You saw him, you heard him, you saw one of the miracles! Would you deny me those sights?

SAM: Absolutely! That is, I would deny them if you're already convinced that he is the One. If you're not convinced . . . if there is still doubt in your mind . . . if the things that you've seen and heard from others are not enough . . . I repeat, if the things that you've seen and heard from others are not enough . . . if you believe that the recognition of Truth and Joy is restricted to what your eyeballs see, what your eardrums hear and . . . and to the unerring touch of your ten little pinkies . . . then run, sister, run! Join the parade! See all you can see! Hear all you can hear! Touch all you can touch! But I'll just bet you this . . . walk with that crew for a million miles . . . live with them for a thousand years . . . and I'll just bet that you'll be no closer to faith than you are right now!

RUNT: Good point, Sam! Now you're rollin'!

LARS: Angelica, don't go . . . please don't go with him!

ANGELICA [*looking at* LARS *and then at* CARPE *she concludes that* LARS *is really questioning the propriety of her traveling alone with the big-time butter-and-egg-man*]: Have no fear, dear husband!

You know, of course, that I must continue my search even if you are not by my side. But fear not. I shall walk a good twenty paces behind Mr. Carpe and should he decide to offer services other than those of a guide . . . a most temporary guide . . . I shall scream so loudly that a legion of angels will be at my side forthwith . . . and if they are delayed more than a moment I shall with these very finger nails claw him . . . if not to death at least to civility!

LARS: I'm not worried about that creep. It's quite obvious that he has but a single appetite! And don't worry . . . if you want to go . . . if you decide to continue I shall go with you . . . and if we miss the Big Man tonight . . . I shall continue with you tomorrow and the next day and the next until we finally find him. I'll go with you . . . not because I think you're right . . . really, I have a hunch that this guy is right and what's more I think that you think he's right too! But I will continue with you because you are my wife . . . and I love you very, very much.

ANGELICA: Lars???? I've never heard you talk like this before! Goodness, now I am confused. I don't know . . . I just don't know what to do . . . or what to believe . . . or whom to believe in! I've tried so hard . . . and I'm still so lost!

SAM: Come on, sister, knock it off! Real doubt . . . real unbelief is just too damn gutsie to be sentimentalized! Until that pretty, little lower lip stops quivering and your gut starts bleeding don't talk about doubt and unbelief!

LARS: Easy, fella, easy!

SAM: O.K. . . . O.K. . . . but, honey, you know what you believe, right? I mean . . . you've got a pretty good idea of what the big picture's all about, right?

ANGELICA: Well . . . yes, I suppose so.

SAM: You suppose so????

ANGELICA: All right, then, yes, I know what I believe.

SAM: And you know who you believe in, right?

ANGELICA: Yes.

SAM: What????

ANGELICA: Yes!!

SAM: So what's the problem then? Isn't it one of style?

ANGELICA: I'm not sure that I know what you mean.

SAM: Style, baby! You know . . . what you do with your life once an ultimate has been established!

ANGELICA: And what's an ultimate?

SAM: The Absolute!

ANGELICA: And what's that?

SAM: God!!!

ANGELICA: Oh . . . for goodness sake! Well . . . that's all very nice . . . it sounds very convincing . . . but . . . well . . . don't you see . . . he needs me!

SAM: Which "he"?

ANGELICA: Why, the Big Man, of course!

SAM: Do you dare . . . do you have the gall to say that once again? Lady, you've got this "needs" business all mixed-up. [*He points to* LARS.] He's the one who needs you . . . and you need him!

ANGELICA: Well . . . so . . . all right . . . but if the Big Man doesn't need me then what do you think that he expects of me?

SAM: That you live, baby, live! Live knowing that the promise has been kept!

ANGELICA: Live???? But just to live is so . . . ordinary!

SAM: Ordinary?

RUNT: Ordinary?

23

LARS: Ordinary?

SAM: Little lady . . . if you think that life is just ordinary then you haven't really lived!

CARPE: Well, now, friends and neighbors . . . now that we have that settled I'm here to tell you, I repeat. . . .

RUNT: Beat it!

CARPE: Will you repeat that?

RUNT: Beat it, beat it, beat it! Beat it before I show you just how theoretically vulnerable your good neighbor policy is!

CARPE: Well, now . . . time is running on . . . so . . . well . . . ta-ta. . . . [*He exits quickly.*]

RUNT: Eat it, mack!

ANGELICA [*the men are quite apprehensive; they're not sure what she will do; after a brief pause, she walks to* LARS, *puts her arm through his and speaks softly*]: Let's spend a few days in that lovely, little inn and then return to our home.

[LARS *hugs her and just before they exit he shakes hands with* SAM *and* RUNT.]

RUNT: Live it up, kids!

SAM: Well, my friend, I'd say we've just seen another miracle! Come on, little buddy, we've got a job to do. Looks as though we have to bury this mess all by ourselves.

[*They exit singing the following hymn—to the tune of the doxology, i.e., Old One Hundredth:*]

> "We'll dig a pit both deep and wide
> And shovel those stinky fish inside;
> And when this smelly job is done
> We'll offer up a Te De-um!"

What They Didn't Do

by WALTER WANGERIN

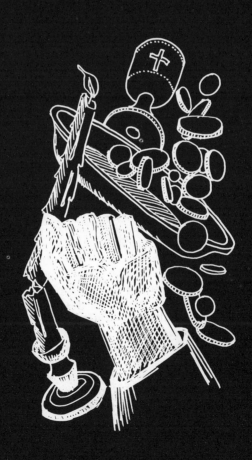

Characters

PETE: The muscle. The violent one. But his violence is not undiminished by some amount of honest affection for his friends. He has little love for the adult world and little thought for it.

JOHN: A youth with deep feelings for his peers and the adult world. He has the perception and moral capability to see trouble wherever it lies, and yet his very morals cripple him before any action to right the wrong.

JIM: A negro with John's intelligence and Pete's violence but without John's commanding morality. He is more angry than lonely. He is embittered about adults but his effort to change them is little more than an excuse for expressing his bitterness against them. It is but recently that he found anything worthy in the church. And that was through John as his friend. He actually had more faith in John than he had in Christ.

Setting

Your own church

Suggestion

The point of this play is to give adults three sides—points of view—to a demonstration. They are totally human sides and should be recognized in the adult world. But adults must understand that to remove any one of these elements not only does away with the demonstration (something they would like to hear), but is also an evil comment on youth. It makes youth less than it might have been had there been the demonstration. The play is also to make something human out of those inhuman cats who demonstrate. The people of the congregation mentioned by John toward the end of the play should be changed to correspond with actual people from the congregation where the play is performed.

PETE [*speaks even before he enters, highly excited*]: Good. Good! Yes, this'll work. I'm sure of it. You couldn't *get* a better chancel, could you John?

JOHN [*preoccupied*]: No.

PETE: It's cock*sure,* that's what. It's a cocksure chancel. [*Giggles*] Anything as old and as sanctified as this has just got to be cocksure of itself, don't it, John?

JOHN: No. Yes.

PETE: And the altar. Oh, BABY! We're gonna work the altar into this, too, ain't we?

JOHN: Yes.

PETE: Tell you what; let's do it to the collection plates, okay? We could roll them down the aisle. Or we could wait until the collection's been taken— and tip 'em over. Yeah. Wait till the money's forgotten, till it's prayed over—or while it's being prayed over, and then tip the money all over the floor; let pennies and nickles and dimes roll all *over* creation. SPEERONGGGG! Dollars, pennies, nickles, dimes, quarters, CARTWHEELS. [*Giggles*] Cartwheels. Oh, damn it, John, this gets me. I can hardly stand it. The whole idea's so beautiful!

JOHN [*replaces a collection plate*]: Sure, Pete.

PETE [*feels insulted somehow*]: John. All right; what's the matter now?

JOHN: Nothing.

PETE: What do you mean, nothing?

JOHN: Forget it, Pete.

PETE: The scheme's yours as much as it's mine, isn't it?

JOHN: I said. . . .

PETE: And you agreed, didn't you? I mean, you *agreed*.

JOHN: Yeah.

PETE: You went along with the three of us last night and you agreed. In fact, you were the first one to think it up, weren't you?

JOHN: Yes.

PETE: Well? What's the hang up now? The altar [*he sneers that word*] hasn't scared you off, has it?

JOHN: You know it hasn't.

PETE: Well, for God's sake, man, what is it? You can't back off now. And we're not exactly Hell's Angels doing this. I mean, we got a reason for what we're going to do—a cause. That's your own word, you know, "cause." And you yourself said it's symbolical; and we're not going to smash anything so's it can't be fixed. Just, well, *you* know. You're the one who said it in the first place. . . .

JOHN: Yes, Pete, I know: a token.

PETE [*fiercely*]: Well?

[JIM *enters from the narthex and grumbles audibly about the church. He is ill-tempered now and nervous about what is about to happen.*]

JOHN: Well, I don't know. We can't just wreck things; we can't just frighten the people. . . .

PETE: But we're not!

JOHN: Oh, but we might. *You* might the way you're going at it. . . .

PETE: Me?

JOHN: . . . We're trying to make a point, not destroy
one. If we're not careful we could just outrage the
congregation, and then what, Pete? They'd never
change; they'd be twice as afraid of change as before, and they would take refuge in that fear.

PETE [*has seen* JIM *rummaging in back of church*]:
Yeah, John. Sure. I know what you're getting at.
Jim? Jim, is it okay from back there?

JOHN: No, you *don't* know, or you wouldn't take it
like this.

JIM [*to himself more than anyone*]: No.

JOHN: Pete, our destruction might breed nothing
more than. . . .

PETE: Shut-up. What, Jim?

JIM: I said I'm not sure. [*To himself again; then*]
There's no real place to hide, especially if we have
to hide the signs, too.

PETE: What?

JIM: I'm not so sure I like this church.

PETE: But it's *our* church.

JIM: I know that; we'll make do with what we've got.
But I still wish there was more private space back
here. I'm not going to drag a lot of signs into the
building after they start the service. We have to
have a little more preparation than that.

PETE: But we *got* a plan; don't we John?

JIM: Details, Pete! [*He begins to walk forward, his
ill-temper transferred to his partners.*] Until every
single detail is planned and in its proper place—no.
We don't "got a plan." We're only half-cocked.

PETE: Hey, Jim, tell you what: this is a cock*sure*
chancel. Did you know that?

JIM: All we got so far is that you and John will barge into the chancel during the sermon. . . .

PETE: After, when there's money!

JIM: . . . You'll knock things over and break things, for attention as much as for anything else. . . .

PETE: John don't think so; he says. . . .

JIM: For attention as much as for anything else! Right, John? Then I'll march up from the back of the church with as many blacks as I can get, and all of us will carry signs. And John knows why the signs, don't you John? So that it *looks* like a demonstration; so that the people know we are serious and not just chasing a sudden whim. Isn't that right, John? So that even here in church we are taking part in the rage that's out on the college campuses, the rage around draft boards. . . .

PETE [*solicitous*]: Hey, Jim. . . .

JIM: . . . the rage that's burning young people up: restlessness and rage against a faceless, inhuman, thoughtless, damnable *System*. Signs. Isn't that right, John?

PETE: Come on, Jim. He agreed.

JIM: To say that even the church—especially the church—has bowed down and grovelled before the old—devil—system. [*Quietly*] Wouldn't you say so, John? Signs?

PETE: Oh, cut it out. He already came around to that, didn't you, John? He said signs are in; but he's bothered by something else, now. What is it, John? Tell Jim.

[*In the preceding speech* JIM *vented some of his anger on* JOHN—*partly because they are deep friends, and partly because he does not always understand his* *friend—*JOHN's *father is the pastor! Now, in this one, the sincerity of the friendship must show through.*]

JIM: Then, after we've marched in with the signs, John will talk to the congregation—because his father is the minister. Because the people love him. [*He looks at* JOHN, *despite the third person.*] Because he *can* talk with more sincerity than anyone we know. And John will say to the people, "We have a precedent." Only he won't mean the signs and demonstrations already carried out. He'll mean Christ's precedent. He'll *say* to the people that Christ did all that he did do in love. And John will mean such a thing because he is John. [*This hurts* JOHN; *he drops his eyes.*] He'll mean before the people that Jesus Christ could turn whole systems over with love, and on account of love. Love. John will say such things behind his words about the temple-cleansing because that is the way John is. Isn't that right, John? [*This last with surprising tenderness.*]

PETE [*silent; and then, abruptly and impatiently because he does not understand Jim's tone or, really, his thought*]: Don't got a plan! Don't got a plan, Jim? What the hell do you call that? Seems you got details enough to kill a commie. Come on, girls; if you want any more details let me tell you about the collection plates. [*He turns to get them.*]

JOHN: Pete has an idea about what to do with the money.

PETE: Yeah. Spill it. Dump it all over creee-ation! And if you guys don't mind, I'll do the dumping.

JIM [*self-conscious*]: I don't mind. Who the hell's to mind?

PETE: Good. I'll dump. And I'll wear the sloppiest

clothes I can get my hands on, hey John? You too.
We can crud up the carpets. Oh, and the altar. I
was thinking about that, too. We can sit on it.

JOHN: You know, Pete, you always start out good
enough. Money-dumping. . . .

JIM: Grubbing.

PETE: Hee-hee . . . grubbing. Money-grubbing.

JOHN: Money-dumping comes right out of the Bible;
it was Christ's trick. But he never went so far as to
desecrate anything.

PETE: Oh, me neither. But I sure wish they had Communion tomorrow. Mud on the altar might not be
enough.

JOHN: Pete, we've got to find a limit.

PETE: That's just what I'm doing; it's gonna be where
the cleaning-ladies crap in their skirts, and the
janitor swallows liquid plumber, and the people
exit south.

JOHN: Wait a minute; dirty clothes are okay, and that
money-dumping. . . .

JIM: Grubbing!

JOHN: . . . is great but. . . .

PETE: The whole congregation'll catch their puny,
hymn-singing breaths. Sure, sloppy jeans and bare
feet and dirty clothes. But we oughta do something
to the church itself. I mean, not just to the people,
and not just to the building, but to the things they
come for, right? We oughta do something to the
Communion, the wine. Then they would listen,
John. Then they'd hear every word you said.

JOHN: No, that's the whole point: they wouldn't.

PETE: They would! I'm only thinking of what you

said Jesus did. He tipped over the tables, but more than that, the little guy chased all those hungry bastards right out of the temple, didn't he? So [*and he begins to play more violently with the collection plates*], well, so it's not enough just to tip over the money tomorrow; we gotta make them feel like running for it, see? Scare them. And when Jesus scared 'em out what did he use? A sermon? John, your preacher father uses sermons. He had a bull-whip. You said it: a bullwhip, didn't he.

JOHN: No. I never said that.

PETE: Well, he musta used something; I seen pictures of him using something. And we gotta use something, too. And *that's* why I wish they had Communion tomorrow.

JIM: Communion, Pete?

PETE [*excited; he has an ally*]: Sure. Sure. What would they do if I started to drink that wine? Or what about this—what would the poor groaners do if I *spilled* it, hey? Or *spit* in the cup! Wowee Moses! They'd know we meant business, that's. . . .

JOHN: Pete, stop it!

PETE: Come on, John. Think what a. . . .

JOHN: Stop it, Pete! There's a limit.

PETE: Oh, yeah. P.K.! Pastor's kid. You are afraid, aren't you?

JOHN: My father has nothing to do with this.

PETE: Like hell. You're afraid even before we've done anything. Maybe that's a good thing; maybe because you're afraid the people tomorrow will be terror-stricken. They'll vomit.

JOHN: I'm not afraid.

PETE: You're cocksure. Maybe you oughta sit out there tomorrow.

JIM [*testing* JOHN]: Maybe you ought to, John.

JOHN: Jim! Can't *you* see where this guy's going?

JIM: Yeah, I can see. He's taking it to its logical conclusion. Push the idea far enough and it ends where Pete is. Where are you, John?

PETE: You oughta know, John. It was your idea in the first place.

JOHN: Not this. This wasn't my idea. And it wasn't Christ's either. I want to change what's wrong here —but *only* what's wrong. I want to cut out a sore before it infects the whole church. But I don't want to deny that whole church. The church is good; it's only *handled* wrong. And Communion, Pete, *is* the church.

JIM: Okay, John; then why don't you do it up right? Use the good. Pray. . . .

PETE: Yeah. Pray to God. Get God to change it.

JIM [*still continuing to test* JOHN]: . . . And do away with the bad all in one shot. [*Very quietly and intensely*] Deny *us*!

JOHN [*beginning to sense* JIM's *meaning*]: You know prayer's not enough. I mean it *is* enough; but we have to do something about it, too.

JIM: We? [*Still quiet*] My signs? Pete's muscle? Pete's ideas? My black skin? Where are you, John?

JOHN: *We* have to do something about it. Prayer can be an escape, you know.

JIM: I *don't* know. It might be getting the right man to work. It's God's house, isn't it? Maybe nobody *ought* to clean it up but God.

PETE: Jesus did it once; let Jesus do it twice; let Jesus do it nice.

JOHN: Pete, don't ever talk that way again.

JIM [*testing*]: Or maybe you don't want to pray to Jesus because that simply doesn't work.

JOHN: What do you mean?

JIM: Maybe the first job Jesus the Christ did wasn't so bang-up after all. Maybe because Jesus the Christ couldn't do it "nice" the first time, the second won't be much better.

JOHN: You know I don't believe that.

JIM: Yeah, man; I know. That's the whole damn trouble with you—what you believe and don't believe. You got Jesus, man, like I never seen anybody got Jesus before. You *love* the cat.

JOHN: Of course, Jim. But three months ago you were baptized, too, right here in this church. . . .

JIM: I love him, too; but you—you feed on him. No, look at me, baby; look at *me*. Too many times you've looked away. Too many times I watched Jesus the Christ cut something out of you. Now you look at me, and you tell me what this "limit" is. Tell me how you know where the good church ends and the bad church starts. You tell *me*—talk to *me*—nowhere else. Pete was right; this was your idea. Only you want it to stay an idea. You listen to that idea whisper in your ear, then you tell us what it said, and I wait to be told. But I hear you talking to something else; and then I know—you're talking straight back to your IDEA. It's a dialogue, man, and Pete and me, we don't belong. You won't talk to any congregation tomorrow; you'll be talking

35

back to that stinking IDEA. And the idea you named "Love." Idea!

PETE: Jim. . . .

JIM: Of course he can't take breaking things, Pete, or fooling with the communion cup, because that's actual; it's not idea anymore. And the signs—the signs are too dirty and too *real*; they bruise his IDEA. Demonstrations, and marching, and honest, smirking, shouting, slapping, punching *anger*, they bruise his soft IDEA. He thought of it first, but now he's afraid, Pete, because he never does anything *but* think ideas. There are your limits, John; not in this church. IN you! Not anywhere in this goddam, cradle-robbing, people-stealing church.

PETE: Umm, Jim. Hey—quit, will you?

JIM: Aahhhhhch! [*A groan of finality, a groan touched with sorrow. He waits, turns, and begins to walk back down the aisle the way he came.*]

PETE: Well, there's no Communion anyway tomorrow, is there, John?

JOHN: No; I don't think so, Pete.

PETE: Then we don't have to worry about it, do we? It was a stupid idea in the first place. I mean about the Communion.

JOHN [*watching after* JIM]: Communion, Pete. It's not just Communion. It's the way you want to do the thing. There shouldn't be that kind of pleasure in a demonstration.

PETE: What?

JOHN: *You* should hurt at least as much as the people who have to change. It's like an operation.

PETE: What? Oh, not again, John. . . .

JIM [*to himself*]: Again and again and again.

JOHN [*anxious about* JIM]: Yes, Pete. Jim, wait!

[JIM *waits; doesn't turn around.*]

JOHN [*approaches* JIM, *then*]: You're going to quit?

JIM: You weren't listening, were you? *You* quit—before we even started. You don't want this demonstration.

JOHN: But I do.

JIM: It doesn't look that way; not to me anyway.

PETE [*impatient; but more than that, bewildered*]: Hey, girls; what time tomorrow?

JOHN: Jim, you wanted to know the limits . . . ?

[JIM *doesn't answer.*]

JOHN: Tomorrow morning there'll be people in these pews. Mrs. Jensen will sit over there and her kids will bother everyone because they fight and then they cry—but they will, all of them, be here. Schmidts and Bohlmanns sit in these pews right here. Harrison sits under any window he can get; and when he doesn't get a window he sits smack in front of the pulpit to let everyone else know about it. Arleys and Riemers sit on the left side. Kraemers sit on the right, with the Johnsons and the Timms. People, Jim; and unless they are sick, every one of them will be here. That's the good. And in front of them my father is going to say Christ. That's the good.

PETE: HEY! Hey, come on.

JIM: Shut up, Pete!

JOHN: And we cannot demonstrate against the good.

JIM: But they've made the church what it is, haven't they? Just because they are the church. And where's

37

Hank going to be tomorrow? You didn't mention him. And Leroy and Linda and Jim? Where is Jim going to be? Jim, who tells you that a hundred Arleys and Riemers never once said "Christ" to him in his own language, never wanted to say "Christ" to him until you did. They're the ones who made the church go sour. They made an organization out of it. It's just a ritual, a closed-up ritual.

JOHN: There's more to it than that.

JIM: Is there?

JOHN: That people come at all is the good and we shouldn't frighten them into silence and anger. That they look only at themselves, that's the bad. And that's what we want to change.

JIM: Look at themselves! They've made the church a club for their own complacency.

JOHN: Yes, Jim.

JIM: Then let them have it.

JOHN: What? Aren't you going through with it?

JIM: No, man! Why should I? To come into this mother I not only got to ask, I got to spread her legs to make me fit. I got to do the asking and the fixing. I got to say, "Please." That's first. Then I got to raise hell to be noticed. That's second. Then I got to show them what they got evil so that they can be good to me. If I got to do it all anyway, who needs them? [*His hands go up; he claps on each count, and at the end he laughs.*]

JOHN: You can't leave. We need you. I need you— for this.

JIM: Yes you need me, No Jim, no demonstration. But you, John [*Jim is intense now*], surely you

38

don't need me. You got Jesus, man. Sweeeeet Jesus.
And the church got you. And when you put those
things *between* people, there's a gulf there. They
make your eyes promise me things you can never
deliver. Friends! [*Fiercely*] For Christ's sake you
loved me. [*Now quiet and finished*] And never once
for mine.

PETE: Hey, wait. Where are you going Jim? [*He goes
down the aisle and then starts back.*] Where did
Jim go? What's the matter with you two? What on
earth did you say to him? John? Did you kick him
out?

JOHN: No, Pete. No.

PETE: Then what happened, for God's sake? I'll bet it
was you John, I'll just bet. [*He moves to the door
and runs out.*] Jim. Jim. Wait for me.

[JOHN *walks back to the altar, replaces the collection
plates, pauses for a time, and leaves by the chancel
door.*]

To Hell with Aunt Agatha

by GEORGE CHURLEY

Characters

AUNT AGATHA
COLONEL JAMES FRANKLIN BUTLER
WILLA COREY
WILBUR SUTSHELL
MARY FROSNOW
NURSE
ORDERLY
VOICE 1
VOICE 2

Setting

An old folks home . . . or so it seems.

Suggestion

Let nine lively young people read over these parts. Then let them spend a day in an old folks home or a state institution for the aged. There let them feel how the elderly are treated. Let the play be presented to the community, church, or gathering where the worth of the aged is forgotten. And then let dialogue begin.

[*Alone, she enters the bare, dimly-lit stage. She walks about aimlessly, clenching a toy doll against her breasts—much like a small girl protecting it from a thunderstorm. But she is old—her body older yet— almost feeble and ready to die. She is* AUNT AGATHA.]

AGATHA: Oh, my God, it isn't! Is it? [*She pauses and looks about.*] It's finally happened, hasn't it. . . . Hello? Is anyone here. I say, is anybody hereabouts? Oh God. . . it isn't this way. It can't be. . . it can't. . . .

[*There is a blackout and a pause of silence. Then the following exchange takes place, with* VOICE 1 *and* VOICE 2 *being young voices, and in the background, a growing rumble of the sounds of old people—maybe phrases, maybe snoring, maybe just sounds. And they build to a roar as does the exchange between* AUNT AGATHA *and the two* VOICES.]

VOICE 1: Now we know you're going to like it here —if you give it a chance.

VOICE 2: Do you hear that, Aunt Agatha? We know this is best for you.

AUNT AGATHA: You know. . . .

VOICE 1: There are lots of people here. People your age.

VOICE 2: Someone you can chat with.

AUNT AGATHA: You mean someone will listen for a change?

VOICE 1: Now don't be that way, Auntie. We're doing this for your own good.

VOICE 2: It's best this way.

AUNT AGATHA: Best for who?

VOICE 1: Damn it! I've had enough of this!

VOICE 2: Can't you understand it's best this way?

VOICE 1: We can't always go around giving you attention every minute.

VOICE 2: You get in the way, Aunt Agatha. You don't want that, do you?

VOICE 1: Can't you understand that!

VOICE 2: We're talking to you, Auntie. Don't turn away!

VOICE 1: You ingrate!

VOICE 2: This way you can die in peace. Die knowing you weren't a burden. A burden for us.

VOICE 1: Do you hear that?

VOICE 2: We're thinking of you.

VOICE 1: Of you!

VOICE 2: OF YOU!!

[*With all the sounds and the dialogue having grown to a crescendo, there is an instant silence—and a pause—as the lights come up, revealing a lineup of old people sitting in individual chairs in an old age home. They are* COLONEL JAMES FRANKLIN BUTLER, AUNT AGATHA, WILBUR SUTSHELL, WILLA COREY, *and* MARY FROSNOW. *All are doing something related to the sounds of old age, with* MARY *knitting and* WILLA *primping a doll—the same one* AGATHA *held in the opening scene—and softly chatting to it, as if it were more than almost alive.*]

AGATHA: Well. . . doesn't anyone ever say anything?

44

WILLA [*to her doll*]: My, I must say that you do. You look very becoming today. Very, very becoming, my dear. [*A pause*] Now would i merely say it if I didn't mean it. Come, come. Yes, that's better—and you're most very welcome.

AGATHA: I guess that answers that. . . .

COLONEL JFB [*after a pause*]: May I ask your name?

AGATHA: Me? Are you talking to me?

COLONEL JFB: Yes.

AGATHA: Oh. It's Aunt Agatha.

COLONEL JFB: Aunt Agatha what?

AGATHA: Just Aunt Agatha. Or just plain Auntie. Whichever suits your fancy.

COLONEL JFB: Ah. I see.

AGATHA: And yours?

[*During the following dialogue,* AUNT AGATHA *and the* COLONEL *try to continue their own discussion, while* WILBUR *is actually in a discussion with himself —though he thinks not—and there is no affiliation with him, except for an occasional glance, perchance.*]

WILBUR: Wilbur Sutshell's the name. Been here 12 years now.

COLONEL JFB: Colonel James Franklin Butler. People call me Colonel Jim, or whatever. . . .

WILBUR: Seems longer than that sometimes. Shorter others. But that's how long it's been, by gum. To the day as a fact.

AGATHA: How long?

COLONEL JFB: What?

WILBUR: In fact, you could say today's my twelfth birthday. [*He chuckles.*] Bet you thought I was older than that!

AGATHA: How long have you been here?

COLONEL JFB: Almost three months now.

WILBUR: I've just been a'telling you! Twelve years to the day. That's how long I've been here. Twelve full years.

AGATHA: How is it?

WILBUR: Oh, my arthritis! Well, times it's good—or better than it is other days is what I should say, I imagine.

COLONEL JFB: They treat you as best as can be expected.

WILBUR: But I feel it special bad in this here finger today. Other days I feel it worse in this one. Then other days I feel it rotting away in this foot here.

AGATHA: You don't like it too well, do you?

COLONEL JFB: No.

WILBUR: Well, of course not! Makes me feel helpless it does. Can't even pick up my own fork some days. [*He chuckles.*] Nor my nose most days!

MARY: That will do, Wilbur.

WILBUR [*oblivious*]: And sometimes I get one caught way up here, and I want so much to go a'fishing for it, but I can't. And who ever heard of someone picking someone else's. . . .

MARY: I said [*she clears her throat quickly and then yells*]: THAT WILL DO, WILBUR!

WILBUR: . . .nose. . . .

WILLA: I should say! Have you no respect for a lady [*then shielding her doll*] or for poor, innocent, little ears!

[AUNT AGATHA *and the* COLONEL *continue their conversation—or at least try—while the others continue their verbal exercise of relieving frustrations.*]

46

AGATHA: Is it always like. . . this?

COLONEL JFB: Always.

WILBUR: I was just making a funny, ladies.

WILLA: My, my, Wilbur. I find it very difficult to believe that a man of your age has never before been told that being obscene in front of members of the opposite sex is not the least bit funny.

MARY: Well, Wilbur?

WILBUR: I didn't realize. I'm sorry.

COLONEL JFB: You know, I'd always believed that old age was a kind of completeness.

AGATHA: Yes. . . .

COLONEL JFB: I still feel the sun's warm—maybe more so now. At least I know I enjoy it more. A kind of gratitude, I guess you might say. And to finally feel the real intensity of being alive and not being able to grab hold of that wonderfulness. . . .

AGATHA: Because it passes by so quickly, and we can only watch.

COLONEL JFB: But here, Agatha—the only completeness is complete uselessness and complete loneliness.

WILLA: Mary.

MARY: Yes, Willa, dear?

WILLA: Will you be finished with her neckerchief by winter, do you think?

MARY: I hope to.

WILLA [of her doll]: She does, too. Ohh, she was so excited when I told her!

MARY: You didn't!

WILLA [confessing]: It slipped. . . .

MARY: And I wanted it so to be a surprise. Oh, Willa, how could you!

47

COLONEL JFB: It's so lonely here, you know.

AGATHA: Even with all these people?

COLONEL JFB: Even more so. You know, I don't believe I've said more than three words to any of them since I've been here.

AGATHA: No!

COLONEL JFB: No. I haven't. But, if you don't mind me saying, I'm glad that you're here. I enjoy talking to a real person again. [AGATHA *blushes with girlish pride.*] I haven't embarrassed you?

AGATHA: Oh, heavens no. It's just nice to be noticed for a change.

[*Thus enters a very sexy* NURSE *followed by a young man, something along the line of an* ORDERLY, *carrying a milkman's basket filled with baby bottles, which are also filled with, no doubt, warm milk.*]

NURSE: Dinner up, all!

[*She goes from character to character with the* ORDERLY *following her closely, his eyes glued to his guiding light—her buttocks. As he passes each character, he shoves a bottle into their waiting hands, never taking his eyes away from his "dream." When the* NURSE *reaches the* COLONEL, *she stops.*]

NURSE: Colonel. It's time for your . . . for. . . . It's time, Colonel.

COLONEL JFB: It can't be!

NURSE: But it is.

COLONEL JFB: Oh please. Not now.

AGATHA: What's wrong, Colonel? What's the matter?

COLONEL JFB: Not now. . . when I've finally found something to make it. . . .

NURSE [*growing impatient*]: Colonel.

COLONEL JFB: . . . to make it all feel worthwhile. . . .
[*There is a pause. Everyone watches as the* COLONEL *finally rises and begins to exit.*]

NURSE: Your chair, Colonel Butler.

COLONEL JFB: What? Oh, the chair. Yes, the chair. . . .

AGATHA: James?

COLONEL JFB [*taking the chair*]: The chair . . . yes, my chair. . . .

[*He exits with the* NURSE *and the* ORDERLY *(of course) following. The others—all but* AGATHA, *that is—shed a few tears, and* MARY *sings a few bars from "Rock of Ages."* AGATHA *begins struggling to get out of her chair, only to find she is tied to it (by the ropes of old age) and can't move.*]

AGATHA: Colonel! Where are you going? Colonel? James!

WILBUR: How terrible. And at supper of all times.

WILLA [*setting her bottle aside*]: It's so distasteful now.

WILBUR [*ditto with his bottle*]: Yes, it is.

AGATHA [*still struggling*]: Why can't I get up! I want the Colonel. Why can't I move. Damn it all! Someone help me. I want the Colonel!

WILLA: Calm down. There's nothing we can do now.

WILBUR: You're simply too old and senile to get out of that chair, Agatha.

AGATHA: I am not! And I want the Colonel! Can't you understand?

MARY: Well, good luck. He's dead.

AGATHA: He's what?

WILBUR: Departed from our mid~ That's what he is.

AGATHA: No. . . .

WILLA: And after such a short stay. Tsk. Tsk.

MARY: And, unfortunate as it is, we must be honest. He left before he was prepared.

AGATHA: What?

WILLA: What she means is he didn't believe.

WILBUR: In fact, he even renounced Him who giveth and taketh away. Quite the opposite of us, I might add.

WILLA: We are very staunch believers. And you?

AGATHA: I believe. [*They smile, as if the victory were won.*] I believe that life is meant for living and that old age is humiliating to death. And this place. It's a hole. That's what it is. A hole!

WILLA: Well I happen to like it here.

AGATHA: You would! Why this place is more dead than a morgue. A funeral parlor, that's what it is. A glorified funeral parlor! Tell me. Does anyone leave here in anything but a hearse?

WILBUR: Agatha!

MARY: Does anyone—young or old—leave life in *anything* but a hearse!

AGATHA: But the humiliation of this! I can't even move from this goddam chair.

WILLA [*shielding her doll*]: If you please!

MARY: When you're old like we are—like it or not —your body becomes your prison. And you just have to learn to accept it.

AGATHA: Well, I can't accept it. And what's more, I don't intend to try. I won't accept it. I suppose you liked it when some twerp of a boy scout helped you across the street. Well, I hated it. When that's the only time people notice you—so that some bastard of a boy scout can do his deed for the day, expecting you to feel like queen for a day—I say the whole human race can go straight to hell! I hated it then, and I hate it now. And then people who supposedly love you stick you in a hole like this—for your own good! Well, I hope they grow old someday and someone sticks them in a hole just like this.

WILBUR: I think that will do, Agatha.

MARY: You just have to learn to accept things the way they are. Simply accept both the good and the bad the Good Lord places in your path.

AGATHA: Shut up, you gutless swine! Shut up! All of you! Shut up!!

[*Thus enters the* NURSE, *disrumpled and trying to smooth her hair. She moves toward* MARY, *who looks up.*]

MARY: We don't wish to be interrupted at this point, if you don't mind!

NURSE: *You* don't wish to be interrupted! Well, I'm so very sorry—but it's time. And hurry.

MARY: Me?

NURSE: Yes, you.

MARY: Praise God! My time has come. I shall be with my Lord and Maker!

[*Excited,* MARY *rises and takes her chair. She and the* NURSE *exit, while* WILLA *and* WILBUR *shed a few brief tears.* AGATHA *looks on unconcerned.*]

AGATHA [*of her chair*]: So that's the only way to get free of this damn thing.

WILLA: Oh, Wilbur. She shall be so happy now.

WILBUR: Oh, so happy to be with her Maker.

WILLA: And her Redeemer, don't forget.

WILBUR: Yes. Her Maker and her Redeemer.

WILLA: Her God.

WILBUR: And our God.

BOTH: A-Men.

WILLA [*after a pause*]: Time goes by so quickly, doesn't it, Wilbur.

WILBUR: So very quickly. Why, Willa, do you realize that I've been here thirteen years to the day now!

WILLA: Really. . . .

WILBUR: Why one could say today's my thirteenth birthday. And I bet I don't look a day over a hundred. [*He chuckles.*]

NURSE [*walking through*]: Visiting hours will begin in five minutes.

WILLA [*primping her doll*]: We'll have you looking as pretty as a picture in just a minute, my sweets. And just think how impressed all the visitors will be. "Such a pretty little child" they'll say.

WILBUR [*to* AGATHA]: Why don't you ever get any visitors?

AGATHA: The same reason as you, I imagine. And her, too.

WILBUR [*contemplating*]: Ah yes. That's probably true, it is. The young haven't much time for us, have they?

AGATHA: Fine observation, Wilbur. Fine observation.

NURSE [*walking through*]: Visiting hours are now officially over. Done with. So would everyone please leave, except for the inmates . . . I mean, the patients. . . . Oh, what's the difference. You know what I mean!

WILLA [*whispering*]: Wilbur, I don't like to say this. But, you know, that nurse is a little bitch.

WILBUR [*of the doll*]: Willa!

WILLA: It's all right. She's sleeping.

[*Again enter the* NURSE, *this time once again with the* ORDERLY, *same as before—only this time he picks up the bottles. And, same as before, his eyes are glued to her formidable flanks. The* NURSE *stops at* WILBUR's *back.*]

NURSE: Come, Mr. Sutshell. It's your turn. And don't forget the chair.

[*They all three exit. Without a word, at that.*]

WILLA: My, they're getting more impersonal all the time. But at least he was a believer. [*She begins chatting with her doll as* AGATHA *does not give the waited reply.*]

AGATHA: She can't hear you, you know.

WILLA: Of course I know! And so what if she can't.

AGATHA: Well, such activity—in the eyes of a majority of headshrinkers, of course—would classify you as mentally unbalanced. Disturbed. Kooky. Crazy!

WILLA: So what. At least someone needs me. More than you can say, I'd wager! At least there's always someone there whenever I want there to be. And always smiling at that. Just look at that smile. Makes your heart warm, doesn't it?

NURSE [*making for* WILLA]: Three down and two to go. [*Under her youthful breath, that is.*] Miss Willa Corey is which one of you?

AGATHA: Certainly not me. I'm no "Miss." No old maid am I, by gum!

WILLA: Tis I. As pure and clean in the sight of my

Maker as the day I was born. And thus I shall leave as I came—pure and unclean. I mean, pure and clean. . . .

AGATHA: And merely half a woman.

NURSE: Come on. It's your turn, and we don't have all day. [WILLA *rises, taking her chair and her doll.*] I'm sorry, but you'll have to leave your doll.

WILLA: Oh no!

NURSE: Oh yes. Remember: we bring nothing into the world and take nothing with us.

WILLA: Oh. . . yes. . . .

AGATHA: Save all the days we have lived, all the troubles we have seen, all the love we have felt— and all the hatred. . . .

[*With doll in hand,* WILLA *nonverbally asks the* NURSE *if she may give the doll to* AGATHA. *After short mental debate, the* NURSE *gives her nonverbal permission.*]

WILLA: I may?

NURSE: It's a bit irregular, but go ahead. Just make it quick. You're not suupposed to converse after you're . . . Go on!

WILLA: Agatha, would you be kind enough to take care of her for me—now that I must. . . go. . . .

AGATHA [*on the spot*]: Oh, Willa. I don't know if I want to. It would be such a bother. [*She realizes what she has just said about herself.*] I'm sorry, Willa. Yes, I'd be more than glad to.

WILLA: Thank you. [*She and the* NURSE *exit, but as she does:*] Her name's Ginger.

[AUNT AGATHA *is left alone—completely alone—with the doll clenched against her breasts. She then holds it out at arm's length, and after a moment of silence, brings it back to her bosom. She begins to talk, seemingly growing younger with each word.*]

AGATHA: Yes, you are pretty. . . Ginger. But I want to tell you something—something from an old woman that I hope you'll remember. Your time will come to grow as old as I have, maybe older perhaps. And it's rather strange, you know. You won't think of yourself as growing old. Watching years go by, yes, but not growing old. And it happens so suddenly, that you don't realize it until it's already happened. Funny, isn't it? And then there's nothing. People don't want you around anymore. They don't want you in their precious way. They don't even care— until your time has come. And then it's too late— for them and for you. Yes, Ginger, even for you the time will come. Your hair will begin to fall from your worn scalp and your joints will become creaky and sticky from use. And then someone will decide you're no good to them anymore, and they'll throw you out. Or maybe, like me, they'll pass you on to someone else—someone who cares even less. A sort of hand-me-down. You know. And what's really funny is you won't feel any older until that happens. Until no one wants you or needs you anymore. Yes, you'll still feel young inside until no one feels you're worth even handing down. And that's when you finally grow really old. And it happens without even knowing it.

NURSE [*having entered*]: Are you ready?

AGATHA: Yes. The Colonel waits for me.

NURSE: The Colonel?

AGATHA: Yes. I'd much rather be with him than any-one else. He made me feel wanted. That's what I need. I want the Colonel. [*She rises, holding the doll firmly to her.*]

NURSE: You'll have to leave the doll, Aunt Agatha.

AGATHA: I will not. Absolutely NO!

NURSE: I'll say it once more. You can't take the doll.

AGATHA: Well, then I won't go. Either she comes, too, or I don't leave.

NURSE: I'll tell you what. I'll look after her!

AGATHA: Don't give me that garbage. I refuse to leave unless she goes with me. Do you hear that!

NURSE: Well. . . all right. But don't you dare tell a soul—living or dead!

AGATHA: Oh, thank you. Thank you! And you have my word!

NURSE: Come on then.

[*The* NURSE *picks up the chair and exits with* AUNT AGATHA *at her heels. But halfway out* AGATHA *stops and looks about the bare stage, the lights dimming to replica the opening scene.*]

AGATHA: It's finally happened, hasn't it. But I don't care—as long as I'm not alone anymore. As long as someone will want me around. As long as I can be with the Colonel. [*As she exits*] As long . . . as I . . . won't be . . . alone. . . .

Sacrifice
to Virtue

by WARREN KLIEWER

Characters

JUDITH HUNT
REV. FREDERICK MERRITT

Setting

The study of Rev. Merritt. It is a Saturday afternoon.
The pastor is in the middle of a conversation with
Judy Hunt, a college freshman.

Suggestion

This play can spark a fresh discussion of youth and
its church. The issues of morality and love, fear and
forgiveness, listening and understanding, and the gap
between people who think they know each other.
Let this play happen in church and let the effects of
it be worked out in forgiving love.

MERRITT: What did you say?

JUDY: I told him . . . yes.

MERRITT: And did you . . . follow through?

JUDY: Of course.
I promised.

MERRITT: A promise can be broken.
That's no excuse.

JUDY: I didn't want
To break or to excuse my keeping
That promise. After all, I chose
Quite freely to say yes.

MERRITT: I see.
Where did it happen?

JUDY: In his car.

MERRITT: Even more sordid than I thought.

JUDY: Please. . . .

MERRITT: What do you want, a pat on the back?
Maybe you want me to applaud
Because you've lost your virginity?

JUDY: I didn't come here for a bath
Of acid.

MERRITT: Sarcasm is a way
Of telling you I disapprove.

JUDY: Just say it, please. Don't hint.

MERRITT: All right.
I'll tell you flatly it was wrong.
I will not tell you that I'm modern,
That I condone, I understand

59

The beautiful demands of blood
And wiggling nerve-ends, and everything's
All right so long as you're in love.
Because I do not understand it.
Love is not love if it sneaks off
To the back seat of a parked car.
This was a sin.

JUDY: And yet I love him.

MERRITT: How could you? Rather, how can you say it?
  Not love. He was exploiting you.

JUDY: Don't say that. You don't even know
  His name.

MERRITT: No, but I know his kind.

JUDY: He's honest. And he's very gentle.

MERRITT: Who is he?

JUDY: No, I shouldn't say.

MERRITT: Then is he someone I know?

JUDY [*hesitating*]:   Yes.

MERRITT: I want to talk with both of you.

JUDY: You shouldn't ask that, Reverend Merritt.

MERRITT: Why not? Is he afraid of me?

JUDY: He doesn't know I came to see you.

MERRITT: When did it happen?

JUDY: Thursday night.

MERRITT: Two days ago. What's happened since
  then?

JUDY: On Friday morning I went to class,
  Ate in the dormitory, packed,
  And then came home.

MERRITT: Alone?

JUDY: By bus.
  Today I'm here. Talking to you.

MERRITT: Not listening, though.

JUDY: What more shall I do?

MERRITT: You came and asked for my opinion.
    I've told you it's a sin. You started
    To tell me a story. But you haven't
    Finished.

JUDY: What else?

MERRITT: His name.

JUDY: It wouldn't
    Be fair.

MERRITT: And what you plan to do.

JUDY: I beg your pardon?

MERRITT: Do you plan
    To see him again?

JUDY: Why, yes.

MERRITT: How soon?

JUDY: Tomorrow evening.

MERRITT: Break it off.

JUDY: I can't.

MERRITT: You can't do otherwise.
    It's clear—to me if not to you—
    Exactly what you mean to him.
    You're not a human being now,
    You're not a girl now, not a friend,
    Not someone he can share his thoughts
    And frailties with. So break it off.
    Never, never see him again.
    You've become an object in his car,
    A slinky creature that says yes,
    The subject of a funny story—
    Let's try to imagine what he said
    When he got back to his dormitory

61

Last Thursday night. "I had this girl,"
He'd tell a roomful of his friends,
"This girl who. . . ." Perhaps he wouldn't call you
A girl but rather "doll" or "babe."
Or "thing." Or maybe even "broad."

JUDY: Please stop!

MERRITT: I might be telling the truth.

JUDY: You're not. I'll tell you what his name is.
[*Pause*] It's . . . [*pause*] William Merritt.

MERRITT [*pause*]:   I don't believe it.

JUDY: Your son. Bill Merritt. Yes, your son.
[*She tries to keep from crying.*]

MERRITT [*trying to speak but for a moment not able to*]:
I'm . . . sorry . . . Judy. You were right
At first . . . when you refused to tell.

JUDY [*she rises and offers him her right hand*]:
Come, let's make peace. And then start over.
[*He squeezes her hand, then lets go.*]
But please don't wallow in your anger
Again. It's not that I can't bear
Denunciation but that I can't
Allow such horrible mistakes.
He isn't evil, cynical,
Not even frivolous. He's good
And serious, kind and warm and thoughtful.
I know that I'm a person not
In spite of but because of him.
I know his thoughts and weaknesses
Because he shares them with me.

MERRITT: Yes,
He's that. But still a silly boy.

And telling me of a hundred gentle
Conversations won't deny
The fact that what you did was wrong;
What I advised, not seeing him
Again, was right. No matter that I
His father said it, it's safe advice.

JUDY: He talks about his father's frailties
As well as his own. Well, shouldn't he?
He knows that you are human too.

MERRITT: What does he say . . . about me?

JUDY: No,
You're not the one on trial . . . now.

MERRITT: I am. There's more you want to say,
I'm sure of it. Don't hesitate.

JUDY [pause]: He's very lonely. Did you know that?

MERRITT: I talk to him.

JUDY: You do, I know.
And yet he wonders if you listen
To him.

MERRITT: I answer all his letters.

JUDY: He says your answers haven't heard
Of questions which, not bold enough
To creep out into daylight, burrow
Beneath the language of a joke.
His letters are full of anecdotes
But there is nothing there to laugh at.

MERRITT: What does he want, then? Do you know?

JUDY: You'll have to sense it: I can't name it.
Listen to what he doesn't say.

MERRITT: If you can't name it, can you hint?

JUDY: It's something like the opposite,
I think, of fatherly advice.

63

MERRITT: You're giving me a hard assignment.
    Why?
JUDY: Thursday night when . . . all this happened . . .
    I have to tell you something worse
    Than anything I've said so far.
    Worse and more difficult. Last Thursday
    We spent an hour . . . no, more than that . . .
    Two hours at least . . . discussing . . . you.
    And then Bill told me all the things
    He'd like to say to you but couldn't.
MERRITT: What were they?
JUDY: That would be too easy
    If I would tell you. Listen to him.
    He told me the things he'd like to say
    And then broke off and said, "It's hopeless."
    An hour or two of sad confession
    That ended with a choking "Hopeless."
    He threw his arms around me then,
    And then it . . . happened.
MERRITT: So I'm to blame?
JUDY: It's your fault only if you blame
    Yourself. I haven't blamed you, and can't.
    Yet you have to know what happened Thursday,
    That Bill was crying on my shoulder,
    Yes, Bill, your man-sized, six-foot son,
    And saying, "I wish I had a father."
    Now, knowing this, give me advice.
    Would you still tell me, "Break it off"?
    Still "Run away, avoid temptation"?
MERRITT: What made you tell me all of this?
JUDY: I had to.
MERRITT: Why?

64

JUDY: You said before
That you're not "modern." Neither am I.
Why did I cringe, do you suppose,
When you described the dirty names,
The leering tone of the boy gone back
To tell his tale in the dormitory?
Because I'd thought of them myself.
I lay awake last Thursday night
Wishing that I were not too big
For spanking. That's why I came to see you.

MERRITT: Well, I can deal with that. Not I:
The church can. And the church prescribes
The very thing you've done, confession.
Let me commend you. This was good.

JUDY: All right, I have confessed; I have
Admitted that what I did was sin.
But I feel just as guilty now
As Thursday. Shouldn't my confession
Clear me?

MERRITT: Of course.

JUDY: And yet you cloud me
With fearful, dark advice—reject him.
Okay, I will reject him . . . if you
Will promise to teach me how to hate.

MERRITT: I'll answer that challenge. What about
Tomorrow evening, next week, next month?
Can you be sure that Thursday evening
Will not repeat itself on Sunday?
And Monday? And next week again?
Have you ever raised a kitten?
Bill had one once, a gentle thing
That, pillowed in purrs and fur, played

With rubber balls and drank warm milk.
One day by accident she found
A wounded sparrow in the yard.
She smelled the feathers, licked the blood,
Within a minute slaughtered the bird.
Next day she brought a squirrel home.
Killing became a habit for her.
Next, rats. She even killed a dog.
Three weeks later she'd run away.
There is no turning back from sex
Or savagery.

JUDY: But I'm a person.

MERRITT: Now isn't that beside the point?
You're not a cat, that's true. You're human.
But if we scratch your skin, how deeply
Must we dig before we find
The savage? What do you expect,
To begin again in innocence?

JUDY: Yes, that's exactly what I want.
Teach me how to redeem my love.

MERRITT: What's wrong is wrong. It can't be argued.
[*Pause*] You two are much too young to marry.
You're much—it's true, don't take offense—
You're much too feeble, both of you,
To marry. Marriage takes more than age
And laws and willingness and money.
Love helps. But feebleness destroys love.
You've not convinced me that you can't
Reject him.

JUDY: I think it's my turn now
To offend. Bill needs me to make up
For what his reverend father lacks.

MERRITT: I'll talk to him.

JUDY: Will he know how
     To use your words? How will you say it?
MERRITT: So subtly that he understands
     I'm wording what he already knows.
JUDY: In other words, you'll give advice.
MERRITT: Giving advice is my profession.
JUDY: Give me advice, then.
MERRITT: Haven't you listened?
JUDY: Not how to reject but how to love.
MERRITT: What would it mean if you'd refuse
     To see Bill for a week or a month?
     Taking just a little more
     Than enough time to collect yourselves?
     Would this be the end of everything?
JUDY: It would. The end of loving him,
     Though not of my being loved. The end.
     For then I'd substitute my safety
     For him. This is the easier way.
     I've thought of it. No, wished for it.
     I wish I could trade dangerous love
     For something safe. But can I? How?
     No, love becomes self-love when it's safe.
MERRITT: All right, self-love. Are you sure you're old
     Enough to take that kind of risk?
JUDY: My body has reached the height and weight
     And fullness of my womanhood.
     Look at my hands. Look at my face.
     My body. They are not a child's.
MERRITT: There's more to growing up than height
     And weight.
JUDY: Yes, risk. The very thing
     You want to deny. And "risk" was your word.
MERRITT: I'm afraid it was. Is that your choice?

67

JUDY: I wish it weren't. [*Pause*] Yes, it is.
      It has to be.
MERRITT [*moving as if to lead her to the door*]:
            Then you and I
            Have nothing more to talk about,
            Do we?
JUDY: I think we do.
MERRITT: No, Bill
            And I do. You have made your choice.
JUDY: And you'll make Bill's.
MERRITT: Judy, I've listened
            For half an hour to your freshman malice.
            But I don't have to tolerate it.
            This is enough. Bill is my son.
            Don't tell me how to treat him.
JUDY: That's all you've heard—no more than malice?
            You haven't listened carefully.
            Can't we agree to stumble through
            Together?
MERRITT: No, the issues are clear.
JUDY: Issues, perhaps. But Bill and I aren't.
MERRITT: I have decided.
JUDY: He said you would.
MERRITT: What's that?
JUDY: Sorry, I didn't mean
            To say that.
MERRITT: What are you concealing?
JUDY: Nothing . . . except the things I told you
            I couldn't tell you.
MERRITT: Oh?
JUDY: What Bill said.
            But now I've changed my mind, I think:

I'll tell you—not because I want to
Or Bill's afraid and timid; believe me,
It's not because of what you call
My freshman malice—at least, I hope not.
But every time you've given advice,
Each word you spoke cried that there
Was something you didn't know: what Bill
    thinks.
No, that's not the right place to begin.
Before, I told you Bill didn't know
I'd come to see you. That's almost true.
He doesn't know I decided to
But did know I had thought about it.
I told him about it yesterday;
He tried to talk me out of it.
Why did he do that? Do you know?

MERRITT: Don't ask. Tell me or drop the matter,
    But don't play games.

JUDY: You gave advice.
One doesn't advise unless one knows.
Explain it.

MERRITT: Isn't it obvious?
He'd want to keep his love affair
Concealed.

JUDY: You see? That's what I mean.
You really haven't understood;
Bill said you wouldn't. You gave advice;
Bill said you would—even predicted
What kind of advice you'd give, your tone
Of voice, the weary face you'd pull
As soon as you saw the conversation
Wasn't going the way you thought

It should. He even understands it.
"My father," these are his words, "my father
Is virtuous. This is the first fact.
The second fact: he lets you know
How good he is. The third: you're not
Acceptable unless you're good
In his way. Not some new, unknown way,
Or any other way but his."
That's what Bill said.

MERRITT: Yes, that's the way
He talks—his words, his petulance.

JUDY: Bill even knew you'd try to break
Things up between us. These are his words:
"He'll sacrifice anybody
To keep the virtue in the family.
Or in himself. I've seen him do it.
He used to use me in his sermons.
I was the villain, he the hero.
In sermons virtue always wins.
He's always Abraham, I'm always
His Isaac being sacrificed
To virtue on his altar."

MERRITT: Stop!
You've said enough.

JUDY: "My father," he said,
"Has half a dozen theories of love,
Each named in Greek. He's never tried
Them out, though, and wouldn't recognize one
If he met it on the street.
Because his seminary theories
Are neat and tidy: real love is messy.
A father who loves his son lives through

70

The chaos with him—the broken toys,
Measles, the puppy love affairs.
Dad can't be bothered. He's too busy
Shuffling Greek theories."

MERRITT: Please!

JUDY: I can't stop.
Because Bill may be wrong, I know;
But if you tell me not to see him,
You'll prove him right. [*Pause*] What's your
advice?

MERRITT [*pause*]: I need some time to think.

JUDY: I'm sorry.
I haven't learned how to tell the truth
Gently. I really want advice.

MERRITT: Yet now, when you and he most need it,
When I most need to give it, I can't.
Will you come back?

JUDY: Many more times.

MERRITT: I need to think. Do me a favor.
Tell Bill you talked to me.

JUDY: That's all?
Anything else?

MERRITT [*painfully closing his eyes*]: I'll speak for
myself.
I'll listen to him.

JUDY: Will you forgive me
For being harsher than the truth
Required?

MERRITT: It was too harsh. But, yes.
Oh, yes, I will.

JUDY [*laughing*]:   You know, I feel
As if tomorrow ought to be Easter,

71

As if a day of resurrection
Were imminent.

MERRITT: Which means that today
We're spending an afternoon in hell?

JUDY: We've barely begun to understand
Each other after all this talk.
How glum are you, while I'm already
Thinking about the dress I'll wear
When I declare tomorrow morning
A holiday. But, yes, in hell.

MERRITT: Will you . . . be here tomorrow?

JUDY: I think so.

MERRITT: No one but you and I need know this:
I'll dedicate my sermon to you.
I still don't know the subject.

JUDY: Try that.
It's a good title: "I Still Don't Know."

MERRITT: You'd come to hear it?

JUDY: Of course. Tomorrow
Would really be a holy day.

MERRITT: Tell Bill . . . hello.

JUDY: May I tell him
That you and I both love him?

MERRITT [*hesitating*]:   Yes.

First Night

by JAMES STUCKEY

Characters

A number of people who stood by at the coming of Christ
MARY
JOHN/JOSEPH
APHIA/AZARIAH
KEZIAH/MAGDALENE

First performed at McCormick Theological Seminary Chapel, Chicago, Illinois, Dec. 1, 1961, by the McCormick Players.

Setting

A room. The time is a certain Friday evening.

Rooms are deceptive. One can never know from the way a room is furnished whether it will be the scene of an important happening or only an enclosure to hide foolishness. This room is small and rather dark. It may not be a room in a dwelling at all. It may be only a small enclosed place in a building mainly devoted to some purpose other than living.

Right of center is a crude bench. We cannot see what is beyond this bench. It may be a table. Perhaps it is a bed of some kind. A woman is seated on the bench, her back to the audience. A man stands upstage of her and to her right. An indecisive light shows us only these two people. The woman is singing a lullaby.

Suggestion

Perform this play on Christmas Eve and let the people of that night, when God became human, be really human.

MARY: Layla, layla, haru'ach goveret
Layla, layla, homa hatsameret
Layla, layla, kochav mezamer
Numi, numi, kabi et haner.

[*Her song ends with the laugh of someone who remembers something pleasant while her heart is breaking. Silence hovers over the room.*]

JOHN [*hesitantly, in the manner of one who is afraid of being rebuffed*]: A lullaby isn't needed now. He's asleep. You should rest. Can't you rest . . . now?

MARY [*turning to him; there is an edge to her voice*]: Rest? How can I rest? Oh, I'm tired enough all right. I'm more tired than I've ever been in all my life. The words I've heard, the sights I've seen this past year, and all that's happened today; I haven't understood. I don't understand at all.

JOHN: Perhaps I should have kept you away from all those people, all that excitement. You aren't strong enough.

MARY: I'm strong enough. You did right. It would have been useless to try to avoid them. How can a person avoid people . . . the people? [*She turns away from* JOHN *and lapses into reverie.*] The look in their eyes when they gazed on him. [*She grows suddenly afraid; looks to* JOHN.] I've never seen anything like it. Perhaps they understood. I hope someone understands.

75

JOHN [*begins to speak, but he has no words; he walks away from her*]: No, don't look at me. What can I say? I don't know any more than the others.

MARY [*the edge on her voice is sharper; she rises, goes to him*]: But you, John, you were with him. You should be able to explain. You've been out in the world. You talk with people. Even if you don't understand, you should be able to say something to me. [*Turns away.*]

What about all that's happened here? Am I just to forget all I've heard and go on about my business like any other mother? I don't think so. I'm not like just any other mother. I can't be. I've had to be stronger and wiser than the others. I've managed to find the strength somehow, but I've always known that I've had less wisdom than that child of mine required.

There were times when I thought it would be wonderful. There were times when it was wonder- ful. It was like angel voices and singing and wild, wild dancing. But no one dances now. There are no voices. The singing has stopped. [*Sits.*] It has become quiet and dark and the world seems empty. I've lived through hard times before. I'll live through them again. But for once I would like to understand.

JOHN: Is understanding so important? When we were with him, it seemed important. [*She bristles.*] We wanted to know how we fit into all the things he was saying. But now that he's gone, now that he isn't here to explain, trying to understand seems pointless. [*Goes to* MARY.] From what he said to you and me this afternoon, I suppose he means for us to stay together; that I'm to treat you as mother, that you're to take me as your son.

MARY: But what about the others?

JOHN [*suddenly hostile*]: Yes, what about the others? Where were they? I could have told him they'd run out.

MARY: Don't you suppose he knew that? And what could they have done for him today?

JOHN: They could at least have been brave enough to stand by and show they knew him. They could have given him a little comfort.

MARY: No one can comfort a man hanging on a cross. He was out of our reach. A man on a cross is alone. Even God deserts the man on the cross.

JOHN [*recalling the scene of the crucifixion, speaking almost to himself*]: Yes, out of our reach. Perhaps . . . perhaps that's where he has to be in order to be at all. The things he said he said to the whole world, but we didn't want the world to hear them. None of us who were his disciples wanted it. Even you, his mother, didn't want it. Each of us wanted him for himself.

MARY: No! No, you don't know what you're talking about. I never stood in his way. I've never tried to keep him for myself. Oh, I wanted his love, his concern, as any mother would want her child to love her, but I never tried to keep him for myself.

MAGDALENE [*offstage*]: Mary, John, are you there? [*To* AZARIAS] Come ahead. It'll be all right.

MARY [*not realizing who has spoken*]: No, I don't want . . . [MAGDALENE *enters.*] O Magdalene, it's

77

you. I'm glad, I'm glad. I need you, need you to protect me from my new [*with some revulsion*] son.

JOHN: You know I'm not trying to hurt you, Mary. I just want to . . . oh, I don't know. [*To* MAGDALENE] She does need you. I'm no help to anyone. [*Turns away.*]

MARY [*ignoring him*]: Where have you been, Magdalene? I've been wondering about you.

MAGDALENE [*on the verge of tears*]: Walking the streets. [*They react.*] Yes, I've been walking the streets. I walked them before he came and now that he's gone I walk them again. I've had some luck too. Where is he? [*Calling*] Come on. I said it would be all right.

MARY: Magdalene, no. . . .

MAGDALENE: He wants to see you. Or at least that's what he said. He came up to me after the . . . he said he wanted to see the mother of the prophet from Nazareth. So I brought him along. I'm sorry, Mary. Perhaps I shouldn't have brought him. I guess I don't know what I'm doing. It's hard when you've had hope and suddenly that hope is dead.

JOHN: No, Magdalene, you shouldn't have brought him. [AZARIAS, *who is entering just as these words are spoken, turns to leave.*]

MAGDALENE: No stay. [*To* JOHN] Why shouldn't I have brought him?

[JOHN *gestures toward* MARY.]

AZARIAS: He's right. I shouldn't be here.

MAGDALENE: Nonsense, you're a friend, aren't you?

AZARIAS [*somewhat doubtfully*]: Yes.

MAGDALENE: Then stay. What's your name?

AZARIAS: Azarias. But you don't understand. I tried to explain to you as we came through the streets, but you wouldn't listen. I'd better go.

MARY: No, stay, stay. But not alone. We need more people. We haven't nearly enough. There have always been large numbers of people. Others always stood closer to him than I did. So many people packed so tightly around him that I could never get close. Not at the end—Roman soldiers stood closer to him than I did—and not even at the beginning. The beginning. . . .

[*The lights grow dim,* MARY's *voice loses some of the harshness of age, her face seems to become younger. As the lights come up again we no longer see an aged woman who has just lost her son, but a young woman who has just given birth. With her is an aging husband who understands little of what has just happened but who is infinitely patient with the young woman who is his wife. She gasps. The lights come up, somewhat brighter than they have been.*]

MARY: Oh, Joseph stay close to me. [JOSEPH *goes to her.*] Don't let any more people come. What do they want with our child?

JOSEPH: Mary. Mary, be calm. They mean no harm. They come only to look at him, to admire him as people will admire a new child.

MARY: But how did they know, who told them? Why should they be so interested in this child?

JOSEPH: How do people ever find out about such things? Keziah must have told them. You saw how tender she was with the child and with you. You heard her say how beautiful he is. She's just a girl.

She has gone to tell people about the child, to ask them to come to see him.

MARY: But they didn't say it was Keziah. They said it was angels, that there was a light in the sky and music. Oh Joseph, it frightens me. This smelly old stable, our child born in a strange place among strangers and laid on coarse hay instead of a proper cradle, and all those rough men standing about looking at him.

JOSEPH: The child doesn't seem to mind. See how quietly he lies there.

MARY: Yes, he's a good baby. [*She sings.*]

Layla, layla, haru'ach goveret
Layla, layla, homa hatsameret
Layla, layla, kochav mezamer
Numi, numi, kabi et haner.

[*After the second line of the song,* KEZIAH *enters. With her is the innkeeper who allowed the new parents to stay in his stable. They remain at one side, out of hearing of* MARY *and* JOSEPH.]

APHIA [*impatiently, over the singing*]: Yes, yes, Keziah. It's a lovely sight. I'm sure the child is more beautiful than any other child, and the mother even more beautiful than he. [*The lullaby ends. For a moment he forgets himself.*] The lullaby, the lullaby is nice. My wife sang it to our children—but not so beautifully. [*Remembering his position.*] But we have no time to be standing here being foolish over a child. We must see to our guests.

KEZIAH [*somewhat cautiously*]: The guests are all asleep now. They'll be all right until morning.

APHIA: But the kitchen, the. . . .

KEZIAH: I'll take care of all that. There's plenty of time, and I'm not at all tired. Please come. I want you to see the baby and to talk to the people you have bedded in your stable.

APHIA: Very well, very well. But it's a sad day when the master is commanded by his servant. If I were like the other innkeepers, I would whip you for such impertinence.

KEZIAH: Shh. You'll waken him. [*She kneels by the "manger" and speaks to* MARY, *with a touch of laughing in her voice.*] Dear lady, here is my kind master Aphia, who has come to see your child.

APHIA: I come here with some hesitancy. My servant insists that I must see your child. I realize that I am not too welcome. But surely you can understand my position. Travelers have been arriving here for a week. Everyone who stops must have a room and have it now. You see how it was with me. People shouting, demanding; I was at my wit's end. And then your husband appears telling me he has a wife who is about to give birth—a woman in labor in the midst of all the excitement—it was more than I could manage. So here I am apologizing. And I really would like to see your child. There hasn't been a baby in this house for some time. Oh, and tell me, the shepherds who were here, are they friends of yours?

MARY: No. We know no one in this part of the country. We're from Nazareth of Galilee.

JOSEPH: My wife and I thought perhaps *you* could explain why the shepherds came. Mary was rather upset by them.

APHIA: No need to let them upset you. You know

how shepherds are. Out there alone on the hillside week after week—I think it begins to affect their mind. I heard them mumbling something about a light and angels.

KEZIAH [*rises*]: I spoke to one of them. He said the angels told them that a "deliverer" was born here and that they should come to see him.

APHIA: Ah, what did I tell you: the fantasies of madmen. A deliverer! He is a dear child, and a sweet child, but a deliverer!

MARY: No! No, I seem to remember. . . .

JOSEPH: To remember what, my dear?

MARY: Oh, nothing, nothing. A dream I had. Only a dream.

KEZIAH: Please tell us. I don't think the shepherds are mad. They didn't talk like madmen. They talked like men who had seen something they had never seen before, but they talked like men who had really seen it. They were frightened, and yet they were strangely calm. They looked as though they had heard a word from God himself.

APHIA: Oh, I'm sure. Yes, my dear, God is always speaking to shepherds in the middle of the night. How can you be so foolish? If God has something to say, don't you think he'd say it to our rabbi who studies the Holy Scriptures night and day? Why would he waste angels and bright lights and music on ignorant shepherds?

This is all nonsense. And it isn't even new nonsense. It's the same old foolishness people have been spouting ever since that madman Judas Maccabaeus. Someone is always looking for another strong warrior to arise and liberate us; for a savior who will free us from the Romans and return our nation to its former greatness. Nonsense! We should be glad that the Romans are generally decent. We're allowed to live our lives, practice our religion, and even make a small profit now and then. If that must be enough for us, then let it be enough. And no more talk of deliverers.

KEZIAH: Please, just one more word. You have always been kind to me.

[APHIA *reluctantly nods assent.*]

KEZIAH: Maybe the shepherds are hoping for another Judas Maccabaeus. But as for God speaking to shepherds, or rabbis, or even serving girls, I'm sure I don't know who he speaks to, but I'm sure that if he wanted to speak to anyone at all, he could do it.

You didn't see those shepherds as closely as I did. . . . Perhaps you'd feel no differently if you had seen them closely. [*Realizing she is being impertinent*] I mean it's possible that you have become so cautious, so careful in dealing with people—well, maybe it takes a certain lack of caution to hear when God speaks. [*Growing more excited*] That may be why the shepherds were chosen, why I feel that God has something special in mind for this baby.

APHIA: Keziah, Keziah, you're becoming all excited over nothing. Think what you will about this matter, but don't you see that you're upsetting this young woman. Please . . . have some consideration for her.

MARY: It's all right. Let her speak. What she says

seems in some way to make sense to me even though it frightens me. It makes me remember things I don't want to remember, things I don't understand. Oh, Joseph, is this our . . .?

JOSEPH: Is this what, my dear?

MARY: No. Never mind. We've worried over that before. Keziah, what did you mean when you said that God has something special in mind for my baby?

APHIA: The girl didn't know what she was saying. You see how emotional she is. She often talks without thinking.

KEZIAH: I know I'm foolish and that I talk too much and too boldly. But tonight, tonight isn't the same. The shepherds spoke of a Savior, a Messiah. I'm not sure they knew what they meant. . . .

APHIA: Of course they didn't.

KEZIAH [*not noticing the interruption*]: . . . I don't know, myself, what a deliverer is except that I know it's something good.

APHIA: Good? Good for what? For delivering you from your work?

KEZIAH: Maybe! At least from all those things that keep us apart. You see, I don't really know you. And you don't really know me. Yes, I wonder . . . I wonder if he could make it possible for us to understand one another. I wonder if he could make it possible for us to understand God.

APHIA: Now that's enough. That's blasphemy. I may not be a very religious man, but I know that's blasphemy. We are not to understand God, we are to worship him. God is far too busy running the universe to bother explaining himself to every little bird of a girl that comes pecking at him. Now be off with you. [KEZIAH *moves toward the door.*] Draw some water for the kitchen. It will soon be morning and we have work to do.

KEZIAH [*abashed*]: Yes, I'm sorry. I'm taking advantage of your kindness. But there is something different about this night and something special about this child. I don't know what it is. Perhaps I never will, but even if I don't understand, I will always remember. [*To* MARY] I'll come back to you later with some food and wine. You must be hungry.

[APHIA *clears his throat.* KEZIAH *leaves.*]

JOSEPH [*going to* APHIA]: The girl has been good to us. We are grateful. I hope we haven't interfered too much with her work.

[APHIA *speaks at times to* JOSEPH *and at times more to himself. He moves somewhat freely about.* JOSEPH *fixes his attention on the innkeeper, reacting quietly to all that he says.* MARY *sits with her back to the audience hearing, but showing no reaction.*]

APHIA: Of course not. It's all right. You mustn't take me too seriously. I have to be somewhat gruff with the child or she would chatter all evening. She's never been so persistent. I don't know what to make of all her talk. I'm not one to put much stock in signs and lights in the sky. But what she said about listening to one another, about understanding God, about a deliverer—I don't know. This world of ours needs something, that's certain.

These are hard days to live in. Life doesn't mean much. Why, do you know I haven't stopped to talk with anyone like this in . . . in years. No one seems interested. Everyone is busy with his own concerns. We don't live anymore.

If this child of yours wants to do something, let him teach us how to live: Jews, Romans, all of us. [*After a long pause*] I'm sorry . . . I never. . . .

MARY [*turning to* APHIA]: You want that from a child, from my baby.

JOSEPH: This child can't do that. Only God can do that.

MARY [*her patience is wearing thin*]: I'm sorry, but I'll have to ask you to leave. It's time this child was fed, this child whom you want to change the world.

JOSEPH: Mary, don't be. . . .

MARY: And you might go too, Joseph. I would like to be alone with my child. Is that too much for a mother to ask, a few moments alone with her own child?

JOSEPH: Of course not. I'll go. I'll be right outside. [*He and* APHIA *move toward the doorway.*]

KEZIAH [*calling from offstage*]: More shepherds are coming! Coming to see the deliverer!

MARY [*desperately*]: No! Don't let them in. Don't let anyone in. Keep them away from my baby, my child.

[*The lights dim again. When they come up the scene is as it was earlier.*]

MARY: Oh God, protect my child from these people. [*With revulsion*] People. [*She loses herself in thoughts and is oblivious to the conversation that follows.*]

MAGDALENE: Mary. Mary, it's all right. It's only me, Magdalene. Why is she acting so strangely?

JOHN: I don't know. Perhaps it's my fault. I did speak rather harshly to her.

AZARIAS: No, it's me. I said I shouldn't come here. Why wouldn't you listen to me?

MAGDALENE: I couldn't listen. My mind was too full. When you said you wanted to see . . . his mother. Well, why shouldn't you see her?

AZARIAS: But I've no right. Don't you see? I was one of those who stood in the crowd.

[MARY *has been bent over. At this statement she sits up sharply and pays close attention to what follows.*]

AZARIAS: I was one of those responsible for the . . . [*letting it rush out*] I wanted them to kill him.

MARY [*rising suddenly and speaking venomously*]: Then you're one of those people. You're one of them. [*She sobs.*] Oh God, God! They wanted to take him from me from the beginning and now they've succeeded. He's gone, and all his talk of love and forgiveness is gone with him.

JOHN [*he can restrain himself no longer; he explodes suddenly and sharply*]: Mary! [*A long pause*] That's enough.

[MARY *is shocked. She can't believe anyone would dare use such a tone with her. She begins to speak— to give* JOHN *a taste of what she has just given* AZARIAS *—but she thinks better of it and sits waiting, some-what apprehensively, to hear what more* JOHN *will say to her.*]

JOHN [*taken aback by his own boldness, but deter-mined to have his say, nevertheless; he speaks*

87

somewhat quietly, but firmly]: Your son is gone, Mary. My friend, my teacher is gone. But what he came to do isn't finished. I don't know what's going to happen now—maybe nothing. But whatever is going to happen will come out of what took place this afternoon.

MARY: Nothing can come of hate but more hate.

AZARIAS [*all eyes focus on him; he is very uncomfortable, but he can no longer keep silent*]: I'm sorry, but I must speak. You see, I know what it is to hate. I know it better than any of you. But I also know what it is not to hate. I think I learned that for the first time today.

[MARY *turns away.*]

MAGDALENE [*goes to her*]: I know it's hard for you, but try to listen to this man. He seems to have seen something that none of us was able to see.

AZARIAS: I thought I was a strong man, standing in that crowd this afternoon. I felt very brave. "Kill him," I shouted. And then . . . I saw him, and I saw myself: saw how rotten I was; saw I was weak, not strong at all. There was no bravery, no courage in that crowd. Courage was nailed to a cross.

[MARY *winces, is on the verge of tears, but controls herself and continues to listen.*]

AZARIAS: If he had shouted at us, if he had cursed us, I could have taken that. But his silence; the way he acted as if what was happening had to happen, the way none of it seemed to surprise him: it was as if he'd lived his whole life for that moment. We didn't kill him. Oh, he's dead all right, but we didn't kill him. He killed us. He killed our hate.

Right now it looks as if we win. But I don't believe that lonely man on the cross is finished with us yet.

MAGDALENE [*looking at* AZARIAS *but not moving*]: Then all his talk of love and forgiveness isn't gone. Somehow you've heard that talk, you've seen that life, just as I saw it.

AZARIAS: No, not just as you saw it. I saw it as one who has no right to see it at all. [MAGDALENE *winces.*] I have no right even to live after what I've done. But what I've done doesn't seem to matter so much now. What he did seems much more important. What happened this afternoon frightens me, because I don't understand it, I guess, but what happened this afternoon—to me—is what makes me want to be here with you; makes me bold enough to come here.

I saw you weeping on that hill and I knew then I had to come. The courage, the love I saw in his face: his power that killed my hate led me here.

MARY: Led you. [*She looks at him intently.*] Others said those words many years ago. They said there was a star—I didn't see it. You say there was power, I didn't see that either. I was busy with my own thoughts when those others came led by a "star." I was busy with my own thoughts on that hill this afternoon. I've always been so busy wondering, wanting to understand, to know. It seems now that I never will.

[*Speaking to* MAGDALENE *and* JOHN] I won't lie to you. I haven't much hope left. Not after being in the midst of that mob, not after seeing what I saw: flesh of my own body *beaten, punctured, exposed* to the wind. But there's something about this man . . . something in what he says that makes me want to hope again. Maybe to hope this is not the first night of his death, but the first night of his life . . . and of ours . . . maybe. . . .

[*The lights go down leaving* MAGDALENE *and* AZARIAS *in darkness while* MARY *and* JOHN *remain briefly in a light which slowly dissolves.*]

It Was in the Stars

by WILLIAM URBROCK

Characters

CASPAR
MELCHIOR
BALTHASAR
CITIZEN OF JERUSALEM
COUNSELOR
HEROD
PRIESTS AND SCRIBES

Scenes

Scene 1: A room in the home of Caspar and Melchior.
Scene 2: A depot in the town.
Scene 3: A street in Jerusalem.
Scene 4: The palace in Jerusalem.
Scene 5: A room in a home in Bethlehem.
Epilogue.

First performed in the Chapel at the Massachusetts Institute of Technology, Cambridge, Massachusetts, Advent, 1968.

Suggestion

This play is a serio-comic strip for the Christmas season. It can be performed with wild slapstick, intense satire, or rich comic flavor. Unbridled imagination can be evident in the dress, props, movements, and setting of the play. Perhaps Balthasar could be a middle-aged girl scout and the counselor Herod's frustrated female secretary. What do you think? Have fun with this one.

Scene I (A Room)

CASPAR [*looking out window through telescope*]: Hey, Melchior, take a look at this.

MELCHIOR: What's that?

CASPAR: Come take a look at this.

MELCHIOR: Did you find something interesting, then?

CASPAR: You'll see. Just take a look. [*Hands over telescope.*]

MELCHIOR [*looks*]: Can't see a thing. It's all blurred.

CASPAR: You've got it backwards!

MELCHIOR: So you have. [*Turns telescope around. Stares.*] Ah—lovely, lovely!

CASPAR: You see it then!

MELCHIOR: See it! Of course, I see it. Sirius was never more lovely.

CASPAR: No, No! Not Sirius!

MELCHIOR: Of course, I'm serious.

CASPAR: I meant, it's not Sirius I wanted you to see.

MELCHIOR: Oh, I see.

CASPAR: Look again—between halfway east and a quarter west.

MELCHIOR: Why, whatever do you expect me to see there! Hardly the most interesting patch of sky, I should say.

CASPAR: Hurry up now. It might go away.

MELCHIOR: All right. All right. [*Begins to scan sky again.*]

CASPAR: Do—you—see—

MELCHIOR: Do—I—see—my stars!

CASPAR: You see it!

MELCHIOR: I see it—but it's most extraordinary! What in the world is a star doing up there? And so brilliant! I say, one really wouldn't need a telescope to see it. [*Looks with naked eye.*] Of course not. There it is. Bright and clear.

CASPAR: Bright and clear.

MELCHIOR: That star is perfectly visible to the unaided eye. Why did we have to go through all this business with the telescope?

CASPAR: It seemed so much more scientific.

MELCHIOR: Oh, yes. Yes, indeed. You're quite right. We must be scientific.

CASPAR: Especially when astrology is no longer generally recognized to be a scientific discipline.

MELCHIOR: How true. How true. [*They both sigh, then sing:*]

THE SONG OF THE ASTROLOGERS
(*Tune: Adeste Fidelis*)

The ancients bequeathed us as admirable lore,
A science long practiced by wise men of yore,
The fate of the future and all that's gone before
It's written in the stars,
It's written in the stars,
It's written in the stars
For wise men to read.

The stars by their patterns immutably do show
The plans of heavens for mortals below
The secrets of angels that good men ought to know
It's written in the stars,

94

It's written in the stars,
It's written in the stars
For wise men to read.

The fortunes of history, of empires great and men,
The signs of the zodiac reveal to our ken,
And all who believe this their life can start again.
It's written in the stars,
It's written in the stars,
It's written in the stars
For wise men to read.

CASPAR: Well, what do you make of it?

MELCHIOR: Unfortunate. Most unfortunate.

CASPAR: Unfortunate! Why unfortunate?

MELCHIOR: It would be a saner world if people still believed in astrology. Don't you agree?

CASPAR: I meant, what do you make of the star?

MELCHIOR: Oh, yes. The star. The star! Let's have another look. [*They both stare at the sky.*] Ah, lovely, lovely.

CASPAR: But what do you make of it?

MELCHIOR: I? I really don't know. Haven't you anything about it in your textbooks?

CASPAR: I looked. Nothing. I thought perhaps in some of those old volumes of yours. . . .

MELCHIOR: Capital idea! It would have come to that anyway. Sooner or later one must turn to the ancient masters. Tried and true. [*Picks up an old book—blows off dust.*] Here's a fine, musty tome. [*Shows it to Caspar.*]

CASPAR [*reading title*]: "The Heavenly Bodies According to the Wisdom of Chaldea."

MELCHIOR: Admirable astrologers, those Babylonians! Now, then—what do you suppose I should look under?

CASPAR: "Stars comma aberrant."

MELCHIOR [*paging through index*]: "Stars . . . stars . . . ," how about "Stars comma extraordinary"?

CASPAR: Go ahead. Look it up.

MELCHIOR: Page ccclviii.

CASPAR: Three hundred fifty-eight.

MELCHIOR: Here we are. Page ccclviii: "Stars comma extraordinary."

CASPAR [*taking book*]: May I?

MELCHIOR: Not at all. [*As Caspar scans page*] Find anything?

CASPAR: Yes, I have it! "Portents of royal birth? The extraordinary appearance of a star, perceivable also by the unaided eye, between halfway east and a quarter west invariably heralds the birth of one who is to become king." Well, who'd have thought! Here's news for you!

MELCHIOR: But who'd believe us? Nobody believes in astrology any more. [*Looks at sky again.*] Pity! It's truly a remarkable star.

CASPAR: Fit for a king!

Scene II [*A railroad depot. Enter* CASPAR and MELCHIOR, MELCHIOR *carrying two suitcases,* CASPAR *carrying all sorts of astrologers' equipment, e.g., telescopes, zodiac charts, horoscope books, etc.*]

CASPAR: Pipe—bathrobe—slippers. Did you bring enough changes of underwear? It'll be a long trip, you know.

MELCHIOR: All packed. I hope you didn't forget any of the charts we'll need.

CASPAR: No need to worry about that. I've checked and double-checked—even brought along the Farmers' Almanac.

MELCHIOR: Good! One can't be too thorough.

CASPAR: Especially at an opportune time like this! Think of it, Melchior! In the company of kings!

MELCHIOR: It is exciting, isn't it! I've never cast a horoscope at a royal birth before. I do hope it will be a favorable one.

CASPAR: We certainly won't win any friends for astrology if it isn't!

MELCHIOR: You don't suppose we'll have any trouble, do you?

CASPAR: Trouble? With all these charts! It'll be a cinch.

MELCHIOR: I meant, with the people at court. I've heard they're very jealous of their prerogatives. Suppose the royal astrologers refuse to let us cast the horoscope! I'd hate to be turned away after all these preparations.

CASPAR: Don't worry. We have a special invitation— we saw the star, didn't we?

MELCHIOR: Why, yes, of course! The star!

CASPAR: And, besides, there won't be any royal astrologers. Their office was dropped from palace patronage a long time ago.

MELCHIOR: Oh, yes. I keep forgetting.

CASPAR and MELCHIOR: People don't believe in astrology any more.

CASPAR: The march of time has thrust aside . . .

[*At this moment, a man,* BALTHASAR, *who is hurrying past, crashes into* CASPAR, *sending charts, maps, telescope, etc., flying. Both men lie in a heap among the debris.*]

CASPAR: . . . thrust aside our noble profession.

MELCHIOR [*contemplating the ludicrous tableau*]: Sic transit gloria astrologiae!

BALTHASAR: I'm terribly sorry!

[CASPAR *shrugs forgivingly.*]

BALTHASAR: Here, I'll help you gather your belongings.

MELCHIOR [*giving directions while* BALTHASAR *piles the materials back in* CASPAR's *arms*]: Careful of the telescope! Didn't break, did it? Don't tear the charts! My books—are they all right?

BALTHASAR: There. I guess that's everything. Sorry to have so upset you.

CASPAR: Quite all right. Could have happened to anyone.

BALTHASAR: I hope you won't think it rude—but just what are all those maps you're carrying?

MELCHIOR: Charts.

BALTHASAR: Charts. What are all those *charts* for?

CASPAR [*to* MELCHIOR]: What did I tell you? People not only don't believe, they don't even remember. . . .

MELCHIOR: . . . anymore. Pity. Pity.

BALTHASAR: Sorry. I didn't quite understand. . . .

CASPAR: Charts. Of the heavens. The scientific tools of the professional astrologer.

MELCHIOR: We're astrologers, you know.

CASPAR [*aside*]: No, he doesn't.

BALTHASAR: Astrologers! You mean . . . like . . . stargazers?

CASPAR: We've been called that on occasion.

BALTHASAR: I'm sorry . . . I didn't mean. . . .

MELCHIOR: Oh, no offense taken.

BALTHASAR: I simply meant that I didn't know there were people like that—like you—around any more. You'll pardon my saying so, but I really thought we had dispensed with—ah—what did you call it?

MELCHIOR: Astrology.

BALTHASAR: Thank you. Astrology.

CASPAR: Well, we haven't!

BALTHASAR [*gazing at* CASPAR's *paraphernalia*]: So I see. [*Pause*] You really think there's something to it, do you?

MELCHIOR: Something to it! You're obviously not acquainted. . . .

BALTHASAR: Oh, I'm not! Not acquainted at all!

CASPAR: And they call this an enlightened age!

MELCHIOR [*To* CASPAR]: Tell you what. Let's cast his horoscope. It'll be good practice.

CASPAR: Sort of a rehearsal before the big show!

BALTHASAR: Now see here. I don't know what you have in mind with this horoscope business. But I'll have nothing to do with it. I'm no guinea pig.

MELCHIOR: Nothing of the sort. We merely mean to give you a reading.

CASPAR: What the stars have predicted for you today.

BALTHASAR: Oh, you mean like tell my fortune.

MELCHIOR: Fortune-telling is charlatans' business. Astrology is a science.

CASPAR [*To* MELCHIOR]: Never mind. He wouldn't understand the difference.

BALTHASAR: Well, all right.

MELCHIOR: Fine. Now then, what is your sign?

BALTHASAR: My sign?

MELCHIOR: When were you born?

BALTHASAR: What's that got to do with. . . .

CASPAR: We must know your birthdate so we can tell under which sign of the zodiac you were born.

MELCHIOR: It's really essential for anyone's horoscope.

BALTHASAR: January 30th.

MELCHIOR: Oh, good! Aquarius! [*Reciting*] "Persons born under Aquarius are quick-witted, intelligent, and love a good time."

BALTHASAR [*beginning to enjoy himself, playing along*]: Suits me to a T!

CASPAR [*to audience*]: I think we have a convert!

MELCHIOR: Now, let's look up your horoscope for to-day. [*To* BALTHASAR *as he and* CASPAR *fumble through the charts*] As you can see, this involves careful research and compilations. [*He and* CASPAR *straighten out their signals, then together announce:*]

CASPAR AND MELCHIOR:

> "A stranger you may meet today
> Who'll aid you in a special way.
> If to his friendship you're inclined,
> A happy future you may find."

MELCHIOR: Not only that—but today is Thursday, your lucky day!

CASPAR: You recognize now, no doubt, that your running into me was not by chance.

MELCHIOR: It was in the stars!

BALTHASAR [*playing it straight from now on*]: You don't say!

MELCHIOR: We do say. And [*to* CASPAR] I think that under the circumstances, we should invite this gentleman to join our pilgrimage.

CASPAR: Under the circumstances, I believe you're right. [*To* BALTHASAR] Mr.—ah—

BALTHASAR: Balthasar.

CASPAR: Caspar here. Pleased to make your acquaintance. [*Business of shaking hands, etc. throughout these lines.*] My companion in study, Mr. Melchior.

BALTHASAR: How do you do.

MELCHIOR: A pleasure, I'm sure.

CASPAR: We are going to cast a horoscope at a royal birth.

BALTHASAR: A royal birth? I wasn't aware there had been [*catching himself*]—you don't say! Where?

MELCHIOR: We don't know for certain yet. It all depends upon the star.

BALTHASAR: The star?

CASPAR: The star. We're following a star.

BALTHASAR: Oh, of course. I should have realized.

MELCHIOR: Will you come along with us?

BALTHASAR [*now ready to really enjoy himself*]: Well —if it's in the stars, I don't see how I can refuse!

CASPAR: Then what are we waiting for? Let's board the train and be off.

[*They sing:*]

THE SONG OF THE TRAVELERS
[*Tune: Jingle Bells*]

Travelers three—One, Two, Three,
Travelers three are we.
  We'll follow the star
  To lands near or far
Till we come where we want to be.

On the road—hot, wet, cold,
Whatever the weather may be.
  We'll follow the star
  To lands near or far
Till we find what we want to see.

Come what may—by night or day,
Our course unswerving be.
  We'll follow the star
  To lands near or far
Till it leads to our destiny.

Scene III [*A street. Enter* CASPAR, MELCHIOR, *and* BALTHASAR.]

MELCHIOR: What an exhausting trip!

CASPAR: Where under heaven are we?

BALTHASAR: If I understood our conductor correctly, a town called Salem-something-or-other.

MELCHIOR: Sign on that hotel over there says "Jerusalem Inn."

BALTHASAR [*with great seriousness to* CASPAR *and* MELCHIOR]: You're sure this is the right place?

MELCHIOR: Reasonably sure.

CASPAR: The star and the charts point in this direction.

[*Enter a* CITIZEN *reading a newspaper.*]

CASPAR: Oh, excuse me, sir.

CITIZEN: Yes?

CASPAR: Could you direct us to the palace? We came to pay our respects to the new king.

CITIZEN: To whom?

MELCHIOR: To the new king.

CITIZEN: The new king? I'm afraid you're mistaken. We have no new king.

MELCHIOR: Oh, but you must.

CASPAR: We've seen his star in the east.

CITIZEN: Stars or no stars—there's no new king around here. Herod is firmly ensconced on his throne.

BALTHASAR [*loftily*]: Come, come, my good man. Let us have none of these cavalier remarks. You are addressing two of the world's eminent astrologers. The stars have informed them that you have a new king. The stars never lie! Now, if you'll kindly point out the way to the palace, we'll trouble you no further.

[*The* CITIZEN, *convinced he is dealing with cranks, points offstage toward the palace, then hurries on his way.*]

BALTHASAR [*calls after him*]: Thank you. Well, gentlemen, shall we proceed to the palace?

MELCHIOR [*defeated*]: What's the use? Didn't you hear what that man said?

CASPAR: "There's no new king around here."

BALTHASAR: Oh, well. What does he know about it? He's probably not at all acquainted with the stars.

MELCHIOR: But if a new king had been born, shouldn't there be general rejoicing. What sort of excitement have we found here? Nothing. I surely expected some sort of celebrations to be in progress. No bands, no parades, no dancing in the streets, no colored lights, no holiday—just business as usual. Why, there aren't even any flags or banners.

CASPAR [*infected by the gloom*]: Not a stitch of bunting on the houses. I'm afraid he's right. There's no new king here. We've come on a wild-goose chase.

MELCHIOR: And I so wanted to cast a royal horoscope. The first time for me, you know.

BALTHASAR: Gentlemen! Gentlemen! Why these gloomy forecasts of failure? Why these distraught countenances—these protestations of doom? Bethink yourselves, gentlemen. No mere whim prompted this pilgrimage, but the encouragement of heaven itself! This is a scientific expedition— guided by the very stars, attuned to the music of the eternal spheres. The sun shines upon our path; the zodiac grants benediction to our search. Never doubt but that we shall find the new king at our journey's end. Follow your star!

MELCHIOR: Our star!

CASPAR: Our star!

BALTHASAR: To the palace!

CASPAR and MELCHIOR: To the palace!

[*They sing:*]

THE SONG OF THE TRAVELERS

Be stalwart then—behave like men!
No doubts distract our mind!
   We'll follow the star
   To lands afar.
And the new king we shall find!

Scene IV [*The palace.* HEROD *and a* COUNSELOR *are talking.*]

COUNSELOR: But they *insist* on seeing you, your majesty.

HEROD: They insist! They insist! Have I no choice in the matter? Have kings no more prerogatives? I don't want to see them! Off with their heads! Boil them in oil! Throw them to the lions!

COUNSELOR: But, your majesty, this is the twentieth century. Such things simply aren't done any more. Besides, we're a constitutional government—the *people* run the show.

HEROD: Must you keep reminding me? Am I no longer allowed even the illusion of grandeur? I command that these men be removed from the palace grounds!

COUNSELOR: Impossible, your majesty. We're open to the public from 9 to 5—and they are the public. They payed their admission.

HEROD: The public! Damn the public! Give them a refund!

COUNSELOR: Shhhh! Your majesty! Suppose they're reporters. The last time you blurted out a remark like that, your ratings in the Gallop Polls went down twenty points! It took us weeks to rebuild your image!

HEROD [*pouting*]: I don't care. The public should be more considerate of the strains I'm under trying to administer such a . . . such a. . . .

COUNSELOR: . . . a delicate office! Oh, indeed, they are, your majesty. I daresay, you've held up admirably!

HEROD [*pacified*]: Thank you.

COUNSELOR: Now, you really must see these three gentlemen. They have come a long way. We mustn't keep them waiting too long. The crown imperial cannot afford a reputation for being impolite.

HEROD: Oh, all right. Show them in.

COUNSELOR: And, please, mind your manners! [*He ushers in* CASPAR, MELCHIOR, *and* BALTHASAR.] Your majesty, may I present Caspar, Melchior, and Balthasar. [*They bow in turn as their names are called.*]

HEROD: We welcome you.

CASPAR, MELCHIOR, and BALTHASAR: Your majesty's humble servants!

HEROD: Now then, what may we do for you? We are prepared to accept gifts, pose for pictures, autograph books, kiss babies, bless marriages. We may receive complimentary invitations to the opera, the ballet, the races, the movies, and grand openings of all sorts. We are further prepared—as far as our schedule permits—to address patriotic gatherings, neighborhood meetings, scholarly conferences, sports' banquets, men's, women's, or family groups —provided, of course, that none of them aims to solicit votes or funds for a political party. We must keep aloof from partisan politics.

BALTHASAR: Your majesty is very kind. In fact, however, we came to request none of those things.

HEROD: Indeed! Well, then, what did you come for?

MELCHIOR: We came to offer our congratulations, your majesty.

CASPAR: On the birth of the new king, your majesty.

CASPAR and MELCHIOR: And we request the privilege to cast his horoscope, your majesty.

HEROD: Congratulations?

COUNSELOR: New king?

HEROD and COUNSELOR: Horoscope?

[HEROD *summons* COUNSELOR *to his side. They whisper hurriedly.* COUNSELOR *keeps shaking head "no" to all inquiries by* HEROD.]

HEROD: Well, what about the queen? She hasn't been. . . . [*More whispers.*]

COUNSELOR: [*shocked*]: Most emphatically not, your majesty!

HEROD: Then whatever is this nonsense all about? [*To* CASPAR *and* MELCHIOR] Would one of you kindly repeat why you are here—the whole story— slowly. We want to catch every word.

CASPAR [*starting slowly and building momentum*]: It all started when I saw this unusually brilliant star through my telescope. Actually, one didn't really need a telescope to see it, but I happened to be scanning the sky through my telescope when I saw it. So I asked Melchior what to make of it, and he got out this old volume entitled, "The Heavenly Bodies According to the Wisdom of Chaldea." I wanted to check under "Stars comma aberrant," but Melchior found the reference under "Stars comma extraordinary." And there it was: "The extraordinary appearance of a star, perceivable also by the unaided eye, between halfway east and a quarter west invariably heralds the birth of one who is to become king." I memorized the reference, as you can see. So we decided to follow the star till it should bring us to the new king, so we could cast his horoscope. The whole idea was to sort of make astrology respectable again, since so many people have abandoned it, and we thought the prediction of a royal birth by an extraordinary star would convince people of how scientific a discipline it really is, and besides we've never cast a royal horoscope before. Then we met Balthasar in the depot, and he decided to come with us, and Melchior saw the star in this direction, so we came to your city and found our way to the palace, and here we are to congratulate you and pay our respects to the new king. [*Exhausted, he flops into Melchior's arms.*]

HEROD: Fantastic!

BALTHASAR: You must admit he makes a strong case, your majesty. It was in the stars.

MELCHIOR: And the stars never lie, your majesty.

HEROD: Counselor! [*Aside to* COUNSELOR] Reporters, indeed! Fools, every one of them. We've got to get rid of them.

COUNSELOR [*aside*]: We'd better humor them. One cannot be too careful with people like these. They might turn violent.

HEROD [*aside*]: Well, what do you suggest we do?

COUNSELOR [*aside*]: I suggest you summon the royal priests and scribes. No doubt they can cook up some appropriate gobbledygook that will convince these clowns to go elsewhere. The fools are following directions from some outlandish book—there has got to be same obscure prophecy in our scrolls that will send them packing to search for their star-king out in the hinterlands.

HEROD [*aside*]: All right. It's worth a try. But hurry it up! What price popularity!

COUNSELOR: His majesty is greatly impressed by your . . . uh . . . discovery. However, since there is no new king here—and I assure you there is none— his majesty is about to direct his royal priests and scribes to search in their holy books to find the place prohesied for the birth of the king you seek. The star, no doubt, brought you to us so that you could receive further help from these learned men of our realm!

HEROD [*cries out*]: I call for the royal priests and scribes!

VOICE [*offstage*]: Priests and scribes!

[*Enter several priests and scribes, carrying scrolls. They bow to the king.*]

HEROD: Royal priests and scribes! These three gentle- men have espied a most unusual star which, they believe, portends the birth of a new king. They have come here in search of that king, following that selfsame star. Since there is no new king here, we request that you peruse your scrolls and find the place—*however distant or remote or far-removed* from our city it might be—where it is prophesied this king is to be born. These men are so devoted to their search that they will travel *to the ends of the earth*, if necessary, to find this new king. You understand our intention, do you not?

[*Exclamations of "Yes, your majesty," "Indeed, your majesty," "Very well, your majesty," etc., from the priests and scribes. They confer quickly, then proceed to chant the following:*]

109

THE SONG OF THE PRIESTS AND SCRIBES
[Tune: Hark, the Herald Angels Sing]

In Micah's book, 'tis plain to see,
Appears the proper prophecy.
From Judah's clan, in Bethle'm town
The king new-born is to be found.
By no means least, from this village small
Comes forth a prince to rule o'er all.
"From you shall come," 'tis written thus,
"A chosen man to govern us."
To Bethlehem with joyful feet
You'll find a king who's really neat!

HEROD: Well, you have heard our priests and scribes.
The new king you are seeking is to be born in—
where was that again?

COUNSELOR: In Bethlehem!

HEROD: Quite right. In Bethlehem. Now, we command you to go to Bethlehem and search diligently for the child. When you find him, bring word to us again, that we, too, may find some fitting way to honor his birth.

CASPAR: Your majesty has been most kind!

MELCHIOR: We go at once to find the child!

BALTHASAR: Gentlemen—to Bethlehem!

CASPAR: To Bethlehem!

MELCHIOR: Bethlehem!

[They exit in a flurry.]

HEROD: Thank God we're rid of them! And thank you, priests and scribes, for a most convincing recitation!

A Priest: Oh, it was nothing, your majesty. Our scrolls are full of prophecies. I do believe we'll have to bone up on our chanting though—sounded a bit rusty.

Counselor: I hope they're not too disappointed when they discover this was all a ruse to get them out of here!

Herod: Imagine looking for a new king in—where was that again?

Counselor: Bethlehem! [*They laugh.*]

A Priest: Begging your majesty's pardon, but who said anything about deceiving anyone? The prophecy *was* in our scrolls—and the scrolls don't lie!

Herod: Oh, no! Not you too!

PRIESTS' REFRAIN:

From Judah's clan in Bethle'm town
The king new-born is to be found.
"From you shall come," 'tis written thus,
"A chosen man to govern us."

Scene V [*Inside a house in Bethlehem.*]

Melchior: Well, his parents seemed friendly enough!

Caspar: But—the son of an ordinary working man!? It hardly seems the stock from which kings grow.

Balthasar: Now, now. Let us not be fooled by appearances, gentlemen.

Melchior: He's right, you know. We have the combined witness of the star and the scrolls. I'm satisfied that we have found the newborn king. I must admit I'm a bit disappointed in the commonplace setting of the whole event—but, then, if it's in the stars, it's in the stars.

CASPAR: I suppose you're right. Well, let's get on with it and cast his horoscope.

MELCHIOR [*to* BALTHASAR]: It's the first of this sort we've ever done, you know.

CASPAR: I was hoping the court would reward us. I mean, for services rendered, we being professional astrologers and all. But under the circumstances. . .

MELCHIOR: Under the circumstances it would probably be more appropriate for *us* to give *them* something. It appears they can use all the help they can get!

BALTHASAR: Marvelous idea! Let's pass the hat. [*Over protestations of* CASPAR *and* MELCHIOR *he passes the hat. Funny business! They secretly go through their wallets, etc. When finished,* BALTHASAR *counts the money.*] A five and three singles. Eight dollars! Not bad—for a start! Now we pass it again. This time for noncash items: rings, watches, jewelry, anything befitting the birth of a king. [*Same business as before.*] Ah! Now we're getting somewhere! One gold pocket watch and chain. One fresh package of imported Turkish aromatic tobacco—good! the father should enjoy that. And one spray bottle of Chanel Number Three perfume—for the Child's mother, no doubt. Wherever did that come from?

MELCHIOR: I bought it for a . . . friend . . . back home.

BALTHASAR: Good, good. Nothing like a little sacrificial giving, I say, to lift the spirits. Now, if you'll allow me, layman that I am—I'll offer these small tokens of our affection when the two of you present the child's horoscope.

MELCHIOR: Oh, the horoscope! Come on, Caspar, let's cast the horoscope.

CASPAR: I'll arrange the charts. You consult the books. Balthasar, if you'll kindly take notes.

[*Lights down, if possible. Musical interlude, while the three men work. At conclusion,* CASPAR *speaks.*]

CASPAR: There. I believe we've finished.

MELCHIOR: Balthasar, would you kindly read back our predictions.

BALTHASAR: Gentlemen, I shall consider it an honor. [*He recites:*]

THE HOROSCOPE

The people who sat in darkness have seen a great light.

For those who sat in the shadow of death light has dawned.

His name shall be called Wonderful Counselor, Mighty God,

Everlasting Father, Prince of Peace.

Hail to David's son.

Blessed is he who comes in the name of the Lord.

Epilogue

CASPAR: You and your dreams! I still say we should go back to Herod and inform him that we have found the child. God knows, a little publicity wouldn't hurt the lad—and I wouldn't mind seeing our names in the newspapers either! We might start an astrological renaissance! Not to mention the job offers we might receive!

MELCHIOR: Well, I'm terribly sorry. I may be a scientist and all that, but when it comes to dreams I'm hopelessly superstitious. All I know is—we can't return home via Jerusalem, Herod or no Herod, publicity or no publicity! It was in the dream—and dreams don't lie.

BALTHASAR: Gentlemen, I perceive here the final great test of your true devotion to science. Your research has yielded results. Your methods have been vindicated, your hypothesis proven valid. Now you must cast aside all selfish desires for recognition and reward and be content with having found the object of your search. As for me, I have thoroughly enjoyed your company, and I wish you God-speed. Now, before we go our separate ways, let us rehearse the moral of this play.

THE MORAL
[*Tune: Adeste Fidelis*]

The strange ways of God confound the minds of men.
What God works in foolishness exceeds human ken.
So if you believe that then shout with one accord:
O come let us adore him!
O come let us adore him!
O come let us adore him,
Christ, the Lord.

Being
the Shadow

by JEROME NILSSEN

Characters

THE WHITE MAN. Middle-aged. He wears a dark conservative suit. Has lots of pens and pencils in his pockets, also bits of scraps of paper on which are memos to himself.

THE BLACK MAN. White's shadow. He wears the same dress as White, but in reverse. Light suit, white shoes, etc.

THE WHITE WOMAN. The White Man's secretary; young, attractive.

THE BLIND MAN. An old man. He uses a cane, has a mask over his eyes. Both he and the Deaf Man wear ill-fitting, baggy suits, the sort of thing one picks up for six bits at Good Will.

THE DEAF MAN. Wears ear muffs. He has a hearing aid in his shirt pocket and he frequently takes it out to check on it.

Setting

Anywhere, on stage or off, where this happens.

Suggestion

Use the symbolism to effect. Work on the double-edged biases of all concerned, actors and audience. For music, Stephen Foster things, like "Old Black Joe," or any other white versions of what black music is supposed to sound like. Be prepared for a violent discussion on what it means to be authentic.

DEAF [*offstage;* BLIND, *on stage, wanders about, jabbing with his cane, evidently looking for somewhere to sit down*]: Hey! Where are you? You got to be careful—can't go wandering off like that.

BLIND: I'm here.

DEAF [*still offstage*]: Hmm? Did you say something?

BLIND [*louder*]: Here! I'm here.

DEAF: My God! Mumble, mumble, mumble. Just because you're blind doesn't mean you can't speak up.

BLIND [*beginning to shout, then thinking better of it*]: I'M . . . here. [*To the audience*] He's deaf as a drum. Well, not that I mean to disparage. Just say that he's as deaf as I am blind. And the best I can do is tell light from dark. Day from night. So together we ought to be a pretty fair combination, my ears and his eyes. That's what the welfare people thought when they got us acquainted.

DEAF [*entering, cutting in, although* BLIND *pays no attention*]: Ah, so there you are. Trouble with you is you don't realize how bad off you are—you go stumbling around and one of these days some automobile is going to split your head open. Then you'll wish you'd listened.

BLIND [*continuing*]: Of course, all their thinking was based on the notion that we'd want to stick together. Close at hand for one another. Once we're twenty feet apart, we're in two worlds.

DEAF: Hmm? What'd you say?

BLIND: Nothing that'd concern you.

DEAF: Don't get smart. You're right next door to death anyway. I could let you get hit by a truck, who in hell'd care? [*Aside, as if* BLIND *were deaf too*] Poor old bugger, if he's got a year left he's lucky. But then he's no good to nobody, not even himself. And that's the God's truth.

BLIND [*wryly*]: Yes, that's the God's truth all right.

DEAF: Hmm?

BLIND: I said . . . I SAID—EITHER YOU TAKE GOOD CARE OF ME OR I'LL TELL WELFARE. AND HE'LL CUT YOUR ALLOWANCE IN HALF, YOU'LL BE BACK SELLING POSTCARDS.

DEAF: Listen, how do you know I ain't got an insurance policy on you, all I got to do is push you off a corner some night, let a Greyhound bus run you over. And I collect. You can't see nothing. I'd be six inches behind you . . . one little push.

BLIND: Well, everybody means something to somebody. [*As he speaks* DEAF *tiptoes behind him, is ready to give him a—playful—shove; but* BLIND *steps aside.*] First thing you've got to do is take a bath. You stink.

DEAF: Hmm? Smart aleck!

BLIND: STINK. You STINK!

DEAF: I heard you the first time. Don't worry. I ain't as deaf as you are blind.

BLIND: That must be a great source of joy.

DEAF: Hell, you don't even know where we are.

BLIND: On earth. In the world. One foot in the grave.

DEAF: One block from the welfare man.

BLIND [*nonplussed*]: Welfare? What the hell for?

DEAF: You thought we was in the park. Like usual.

BLIND: No. It seemed different.

DEAF: Damn right it's different.

BLIND [*frightened*]: You're not getting rid of me, are you?

DEAF: Hmm? Rid of you? What do you think?

BLIND: Well, maybe I said some things. Maybe I offended. BUT I NEVER MEANT ANYTHING.

DEAF: I guess it scares you, eh? You don't want to go into no home.

BLIND: I can take care of myself.

DEAF: That's not what welfare says. Last time you lived alone. . . .

BLIND: I spilled some water and I burned myself. It was an accident. It happens to lots of people.

DEAF: Right on your crotch, you were so damn careless. Oh well, I guess that don't make any difference to you, one place is as good as another. Once a man's your age.

BLIND: Don't worry. You're going to get old too.

DEAF: But I ain't blind. You're blind.

BLIND: You're deaf. You need me to hear for you.

DEAF: I can get along. What I can't hear I can ask people to write out for me.

BLIND: Wait! You mentioned an insurance policy. Well, why not. I'll help you pay for it. I'm old, you won't have long to wait. And then you can collect. $10,000. Isn't that worth it? You can spend it anyway you want.

DEAF: Except that nobody'd write insurance on you. You're too old. Sack of bones. You got snot running out of your eyes and tears out of your nose. You're

so old your body's forgot how to operate the plumb-
ing.

BLIND: That's not very funny. At least I don't think
so. But you go ahead and have your joke. I don't
mind.

DEAF: We're almost there now.

BLIND: Where? Where are we?

DEAF: We're going to see the welfare. I'm turning
you over to them. And they'll put you into a home.

BLIND: What did I ever do to you?

DEAF: That insurance policy, you don't really mean
that, do you?

BLIND: Is that what you're after? Just tell me.
Please.

DEAF: You mean if I'm after it, you'll give it to me?

BLIND: Maybe.

DEAF: Maybe what?

BLIND: Maybe . . . maybe I've got resources.

DEAF: Resources? Yes, I'll sure bet you have. Like a
tree's got leaves.

BLIND: You don't know anything about me.

DEAF: You're blind.

BLIND: I can hear. I can hear things you never
dreamed of.

DEAF [*about to speak, he pauses, then smiles and
shouts into* BLIND's *ear*]: Hey! Watch out: A truck's
run loose! [BLIND *spins, dives, sprawls;* DEAF *laughs.*]
By God, a blind man just don't know who he can
trust, does he?

BLIND [*looking up angrily*]: I suppose you do!

DEAF [*surprised at* BLIND's *outburst*]: Eh? What was
that? [BLIND *swings at* DEAF *but is far off the mark;*

DEAF *laughs, reaches down and picks up* BLIND, *leads him offstage.*]

BLIND [*thrashing ineffectively*]: Don't worry! I'll have the last laugh. DEAF *shoves him along rudely.*] And you won't be able to hear it.

[*They exit; the lights go down and out. As the lights come up, the* WHITE MAN *is standing at center stage, awkwardly holding his* SECRETARY's *pencil and note-book. Meanwhile, the* SEC'Y *is on the fringe of the staging area, in an embrace with the* BLACK MAN.]

WHITE: Damn it! Something's got to be done about it. [*The* SEC'Y, *still in the embrace, pulls away slightly to listen, shrugs, then resumes the embrace*]. I've got to get rid of it. Well, I've said that before; I know I've said it before. But there's a time for action. [*To the* SEC'Y] Did you hear what I said? It's time to do something.

SEC'Y [*sighing, releasing herself from the embrace*]: I suppose. If you think so. [*She crosses to him and takes the pad and pencil from him;* BLACK crosses to stand behind WHITE, to be his "shadow."] My God, you've gotten pale. Don't you feel good?

WHITE: I feel fine. I'm mildly upset. [*A buzzer rings.*] Now what's that?

SEC'Y: Somebody's in the outer office. [*She crosses to exit.*]

WHITE: Where do you think you're going?

SEC'Y: To see who it is. That's my job.

WHITE: They can wait.

SEC'Y: It might be someone important.

WHITE: In a welfare office? Not very likely.

SEC'Y: Did you have a letter?

WHITE: A letter? Did you bring one in for me?

SEC'Y: You called me. You said you wanted to dictate.

WHITE: It's about . . . well, it's about this damn shadow.

SEC'Y: Shadow? What shadow?

WHITE: *This* shadow! [*He turns quickly to grab* BLACK; *but* BLACK *has anticipated and thus turns around too, makes the same grabbing motion.*] Ha! Tricky devil! [*He turns back to the* SEC'Y.] Did you see that? I tell you, he's unconscious. He reads my mind.

SEC'Y: A shadow?

WHITE: Well, didn't you see it?

[*The buzzer rings again.*]

SEC'Y: I've got to be going.

WHITE: I asked you a question.

SEC'Y: Everybody's got a shadow. That's nothing to get excited about. [*She points to her shadow.*] Look. There's mine. "I have a little shadow, it goes in and out with me."

WHITE: I'm not talking about that. [*The buzzer rings; the* SEC'Y *edges toward the exit.*] I'm not talking about a shadow. I'm talking about a SHADOW!

[*Suddenly he whirls, tries to capture* BLACK; *once again* BLACK *is too quick; a series of lunges by* WHITE *also fails, so* WHITE *decides to be more subtle, like a boy trying to catch a firefly in a bottle—what follows is a clumsy slow-motion ballet in which* BLACK *and* WHITE *move in unison and* BLACK *always manages to elude* WHITE, *while imitating his moves as though he, too, were chasing a shadow. Shortly after the ballet begins, the* SEC'Y *exits.*]

BLACK [*suddenly interrupting the ballet*]: You know, man, we ain't getting no place.

WHITE: Who said that?

BLACK [*soft laughter; he whispers*]: Who said that?

WHITE: I said that.

BLACK [*whispering*]: So did I.

WHITE [*turning petulantly, walking away from* BLACK, *who follows him*]: I'm warning you. I've got a plan of action.

BLACK: Is that supposed to scare me?

WHITE: Other people's shadows keep their mouth shut. Other people don't have any trouble at all. And all you do is give me a lot of lip.

BLACK: I never asked to be with you every place you go.

WHITE: Neither did I. That's just the way it is.

BLACK: Who says?

WHITE: See, you're being argumentative again. A man shouldn't have to put up with that kind of talk from his shadow.

BLACK: I follow you around every place you go.

WHITE: Naturally.

BLACK: Well, what for? What do I get for it!

WHITE: I'll show you what you get for it. Damn soon!

BLACK: You're a fine one to talk. Every time you take a crap, guess who gets shit on.

WHITE: Hell, that's just the nature of things.

BLACK [*suddenly full of strange glee*]: Except in the dark.

WHITE: What do you mean by that?

BLACK: When things get reversed. Like a negative. When everything goes dark, then shadows are white. We got to start learning that, both of us.

WHITE [*calling*]: Miss Bright! Miss Bright!

BLACK: What you want her for? Maybe you want to teach me how to give dictation.

WHITE: Nobody else pays any attention to you. I don't know why I should either.

BLACK: She sure do.

WHITE: She's . . . oblivious. Doesn't know you exist.

BLACK: I guess she must dream a lot then. About me.

WHITE: I wouldn't have any idea. What she dreams about. That's her business. [*Calling again*] Miss Bright!

BLACK: Well, I reckon that's a good idea, you get her and finish up this welfare business for today. It's gonna be dark soon, gonna be your turn to play the shadow. Oh man! And ain't I got a whole lot of dictatin' to do.

WHITE: I'll show you what I'm going to do. Miss Bright!

SEC'Y [*enters crisply, pencil and pad in hand;* BLACK *falls in as* WHITE's *shadow, although slyly he winks at her*]: You called?

WHITE: Do you notice anything different?

SEC'Y: Different? About what?

WHITE: About? About me!

SEC'Y: You're . . . you're not as pale. In fact, I think you're a little flushed. You're not feverish, are you?

WHITE: No, not at all. I'm fine. And you say that everything appears . . . is quite normal?

SEC'Y [BLACK *blows her a kiss and she returns it before she responds*]: Oh yes; quite normal, I'd say.

WHITE [*nonplussed, he blows a kiss to the* SEC'Y, *but she responds only with a quizzical look*]: Then there's . . . there's nothing wrong? Everything's according to schedule?

SEC'Y: I suppose so. I'm not always certain what your schedule is.

WHITE: And the men who came into your office, two of them.

SEC'Y [*brightening*]: That's right. Two of them. Two men. How did you know?

WHITE: Two men? And one is older?

SEC'Y: Oh yes, one is definitely older than the other.

WHITE: And they want to see me?

SEC'Y: They said they wanted to see the welfare man. Are you expecting them? They aren't in your appointment book. And they wouldn't give me their names.

WHITE [*smiling at that*]: Hmm. Clever. You never saw them before?

SEC'Y: I don't think so. Of course, there are a lot of funny people that come in every day.

WHITE: Yes, that's God's truth, Miss Bright. A lot of funny people.

SEC'Y: Do you know them—these two?

WHITE [*guardedly*]: These two? Oh, I doubt it. As you say, Miss Bright, there are so many.

SEC'Y: So, should I show them in? [*He nods and she exits;* BLACK *whistles appreciatively.*]

WHITE [*over his shoulder, venomously*]: Bastard!

BLACK: Shit!

WHITE: That's quite a vocabulary you've got.

BLACK: My ass.

WHITE [*making no attempt to confront* BLACK *face-to-face*]: You ought to be grateful.

BLACK: You just wait. Night's comin'.

WHITE: I mean, grateful. I've taken you into some pretty nice places. Raised your level of living more than a few notches. A hell of a lot of good it did.

BLACK: I do my job.

WHITE: At least you like to think so.

BLACK: Well, what do you think you'd be without me? You wouldn't even be white.

WHITE: I haven't the vaguest idea what you're talking about.

[BLIND *and* DEAF *stumble in;* BLIND *is groping with his cane while* DEAF *exhorts information from him concerning who it is they're supposed to see.*]

WHITE: Ah, fine. I presume you boys are the Action Committee.

BLIND [*to* WHITE, *as* BLACK *takes his place once again as shadow*]: Is this the Welfare Office?

DEAF [*smiling all around, shouting*]: IS THIS THE WELFARE OFFICE?

BLIND [*to* WHITE]: He's *deaf.* [WHITE *nods.*]

DEAF: I knew it was.

WHITE [*to* BLIND]: What's he talking about?

BLIND: Welfare. He wants to get rid of . . . .

DEAF: More damn trouble, I tell you. [*Buttonholing* WHITE] You wouldn't know the trouble—not hearing quite right, you get things mixed up. And God knows there are few people in this world a man can rely on. Going to hell in a handbasket.

BLIND: I'm not going to sign anything. And that's a promise.

WHITE [*to* BLIND]: And you're blind?

BLIND: He's deaf.

WHITE: Brilliant.

BLIND: Deaf! He's deaf. D-E-A-F.

WHITE: And you're blind.

DEAF: I'm deaf. But he can't even see. Not a damn thing.

BLIND: I can tell when it gets dark.

WHITE [*smiling, increasingly certain that this is the clever pair he's been waiting for*]: I'll bet you can. I'll bet you can spot a spot of dark whenever you want to.

BLACK [*getting nervous*]: What the hell . . . what's going on?

BLIND: I'm not signing anything. I hope you got that straight.

WHITE: No, no, nothing like that. It's not a complicated deal. We don't have to spend a lot of time talking it over. Just do what you've got to do and we'll settle.

BLIND: It all started out simple enough, him watching and me listening. And then he made some funny remarks—said he wanted to have me out of the way. At first I didn't think he was serious. But the more we talked and the more we walked, the more serious he got.

WHITE [*into* DEAF's *ear*]: The world belongs to the man of decision!

DEAF: Well, it took a while. But now I know what I got to do.

WHITE [*clapping him on the back*]: Splendid!

DEAF: There's just no future in going on like this any longer.

WHITE [*to* BLACK]: You see, action. That's what I promised, that's what I'm going to deliver.

BLACK: Boy, you sure are crazy. You're all crazy.

WHITE: I'd expect you to say that. Any time you come across anybody who means business, *you* think they're crazy. [*He takes a revolver from his pocket, shows it to* BLACK.] I suppose you think this is crazy too.

BLACK: You put that away.

DEAF: A gun.

BLIND: A gun? Who's got a gun?

BLACK: Miss Bright! Come quick!

WHITE [*standing with* DEAF *and* BLIND]: My rod and my staff, they frighten you, eh?

SEC'Y [*entering*]: What's the matter?

BLACK: He's got a gun.

WHITE: It's nothing. [*To* BLIND] Do you see anything unusual?

BLIND [*to* DEAF, *softly*]: What's he talking about?

DEAF: Hmm? Speak up. I can't hear.

WHITE: I'm merely auditioning replacements. [*He smiles at the* SEC'Y, *she smiles back.*] Action is the true test of sincerity.

BLACK [*to the* SEC'Y]: What the hell is he talking about? [*She smiles, shrugs.*]

DEAF [*to* BLIND]: This is a damn funny welfare office, if you ask me.

WHITE [*to* BLACK]: Replacements for you, old shadow, old friend. The gun is nothing more than a gesture. A symbol. [*He pockets the gun, turns to* BLIND *and* DEAF.] All right now, boys, let's shape up; time for a few simple questions, and then we'll get on with the more important business.

[*He shoves them together, begins asking questions: "Age?" "Weight?" "Height?" "Childhood diseases?"*]

"Any venereal disease or insanity in your family?"
"Have you been vaccinated for small pox?" "Do you
have any identifying scars or birth-marks?" "Under
what zodiacal sign were you born?" DEAF *has trouble*
hearing and BLIND *has trouble comprehending, but*
they answer as best they can.]

BLACK [*while the interrogation is taking place, he*
crosses to the SEC'Y, *who ignores him*]: Hey, listen,
what the hell's going on here? Did you know he
carries a gun? [*No answer; he takes her arm and*
she pulls away.] Hey, what's the matter. You never
used to be like this. [*She turns away.*] Hey, we used
to make it pretty good, you and me—what happened?

SEC'Y: You're on your way out.

BLACK: Just a little while ago, I swear to God, he was
scared of me.

SEC'Y: But now he's replacing you.

BLACK: Listen, I never asked for the job in the first
place.

SEC'Y: Asked? What do you mean: *asked?*

BLACK: I was brought in. . . .

SEC'Y: You were nothing. And then you got to be a
shadow. Now you're not going to be a shadow any
more. When you're not a shadow—well, you're
nothing.

BLACK [*he reaches for her to embrace her*]: Listen,
you said it yourself: you said we really made it.
Didn't you say that? I heard you say it. Hell, I *felt*
it; I felt that body quiver . . . I heard those little
cries, little mousey moans.

SEC'Y: I don't remember.

BLACK [*he drops to his knees, crawls to her, clutches her*]: Listen, you ain't had nothin' yet. I got enough to take you 'round the world three times and back again.

SEC'Y [*she slaps him*]: You couldn't even get a passport—since you don't have any name, except his. So if you want to be somethin', then you better get back there and be his shadow. 'Cause that is the most you're ever going to be.

WHITE [*as* BLACK *resumes his place as shadow,* WHITE *concludes the interrogation*]: One more thing: are you afraid of heights, depths, open spaces, closed spaces, principalities, demons, unnamed powers, men in uniform?

DEAF: If a man's not guilty, what's he got to be afraid of?

WHITE: Bravo! Well said. [DEAF *smiles, nudges* BLIND.] The hour of decision is arriving. [*Suddenly he is aware of* BLACK.] Oh, I thought that you'd left.

BLACK: I wasn't sure I'd been let off.

WHITE: Why don't you ask Miss Bright. She handles that sort of thing.

BLACK: You don't expect me just to walk out?

WHITE: You'll get severance pay. I'm fair. I've always been fair. After all, you brought this trouble on yourself. Shadows who keep their big mouth shut never have cause for complaint. [*Turning to the* SEC'Y] Well, what do you think, Baby?

SEC'Y: I like both of them.

WHITE: They're fearless types. Devoted. Sacrificial.

BLIND [*to* DEAF]: What's he talking about?

DEAF: I'm going to get a job. And as far as I'm concerned, you're out in the cold. Tough luck.

WHITE [*overhearing them*]: Wait! Two of you—I brought you both here. So I'll provide for both. You! [*Pointing to* DEAF] You get the job as my shadow. Number one. [*Then to* BLIND.] But that isn't all. Old man, you have a style too, a deserving countenance. Therefore, I shall permit you to be the shadow's shadow.

BLACK: And I suppose I'm out in the cold, just like that. Well, I got no regrets, that's for damn sure. Even if I do starve to death. There ain't much call for a used-up shadow.

WHITE [*to* DEAF *and* BLIND]: I took him, dried him off, he was like a lost puppy. I fed him, clothed him, called the doctor for him when he got the mumps. I smiled at his peculiarities. In return I asked for nothing but a *little* loyalty. A thimblefull, no more than that. A smidgin. The merest sign that he acknowledged all that I've done for him.

BLACK [*unconvincedly, a last gasp effort to impress*]: Listen, man. You know what I said. Night's comin'. That's my time.

WHITE [*cheerfully*]: Night? That's the end of day. The end. That's you, all right. I'm the morning. I'm light, the beginning. You're dark, black, the end. [*To* SEC'Y] That figures, doesn't it? [*She smiles;* DEAF *tries to hear, nods earnestly even though he's missed it.*]

BLACK [*trying to muster up menace*]: Just the same. . . .

WHITE: Just the same—I've got light all night long!
Don't you forget it. I've got spotlights, headlights,
flashlights. . . .

DEAF [*cutting in enthusiastically*]: Foglights!

BLIND [*joining in, but uncertainly*]: Traffic lights?

SEC'Y: Streetlights!

WHITE: Searchlights! Floodlights! Lights! Lights!

BLIND: There ain't no darkness.

DEAF: There ain't no darkness!

SEC'Y: Fireflies! Bonfires! Lightbulbs! Electric wires!
Men on poles. Night and day. Neither snow nor
sleet nor pain of rain. . . .

BLIND: No night!

DEAF: Hurrah for it all!

WHITE: Hurrah!

[*He takes out his pistol again; he shoots—and he
hears a second shot. He turns and sees that his shadow
has pulled out a gun too. The shadow functions now
as a mirror image—*WHITE *tries to shake off* BLACK,
but BLACK *stays with him, no matter how tricky*
WHITE *gets.*]

WHITE: Damn you!

BLACK: Damn you!

WHITE: Nigger!

BLACK: Nigger!

SEC'Y [*it is unclear whom she is addressing*]: Go on,
let him have it.

DEAF: Give it to him!

BLIND [*completely disoriented*]: Kill him, kill him!

WHITE: Devil! [*He aims at* BLACK *and* BLACK *aims at*
WHITE.]

BLACK: Devil!

132

[*Two shots are fired;* DEAF *drops; the* SEC'Y *shrieks, crosses toward him, goes back to* BLIND *and leads him to the fallen* DEAF. *As they are approaching,* WHITE *and* BLACK *slowly—as though in a dream sequence— put away their pistols. But now, in the mirror exercise,* BLACK *is the leader and* WHITE *follows him.*]

BLIND [*to the* SEC'Y, *badly confused*]: What's the matter? What was that noise?

SEC'Y: Your friend; he was shot.

BLIND: The deaf fellow? The one who couldn't hear?

SEC'Y: He was shot.

BLIND [*he reaches out and his hand is guided by the* SEC'Y *until he finally touches* DEAF; *carefully he proves for himself the lifelessness of the body*]: I'll be damned. Couldn't'a happened to a nicer fellow. [*Now* BLACK *and* WHITE *are watching.*] Yes sir, I'll be damned. He's stiffening up all right, getting nice and *stiff.* [BLACK *suddenly wrenches out of the mirror exercise and crosses to* BLIND, *presses the gun in his hand.*]

BLACK: You been promoted, fellow.

BLIND [*clutching the pistol*]: Hey! That's right, now I'm the shadow. [*He gropes on hands and knees for his cane and, finding it, stumbles to his feet.*]

BLACK [*crossing to* SEC'Y]: All that shit about light— you don't believe that, do you? [*She turns away from him, he pinches her and exits.*]

BLIND [*on his feet, shouting triumphantly*]: Shadow! Shadow!

WHITE [*like an echo*]: Shadow!

[*He mirrors* BLIND; *they do a hobbling shuffle—a grotesque dance—as the lights dim down and out.*]

Here Comes the Judge

by NORMAN HABEL and WALTER WANGERIN

Characters

JOHN
DAVID
STEVE
THE JUDGE

*First performed in Capitol Drive Lutheran Church,
Milwaukee, Wisconsin, on Good Friday, 1969.*

Setting

Your home church

Suggestion

Use this play as the point of departure for a discussion with adults in your home congregation about the generation gap. The gap in question involves more than age. It has to do with worship, faith, Christ, and being human in our day. If the pastor or a parent plays the judge an even deeper conflict may become evident. In the process the church with its chancel drama is judged by the youth.

[DAVID *and* JOHN *wait impatiently.* DAVID *is more upset than* JOHN, *but they have the same thing on their mind. The judge enters. He is elderly, composed, and ready for business.*]

JUDGE: The court will come to order. We continue the case of the people versus Jesus of Nazareth. He's been charged with . . . deception. Among other things. But, yes; deception. I think we should work on that one today. Gentlemen: shall we begin?

JOHN [DAVID *and* JOHN *look at each other*]: Your honor, do you really think so? Do we have to go on? I mean, we aren't getting anywhere. Sir, we appreciate your concern for the good name of your Lord and we know you mean well, but . . . the trial isn't what it was supposed to be. You . . . Sir, you're the laughingstock of the community! I don't like to say it, but it's true. . . .

DAVID: I agree. At first I thought this trial was a great idea. It was honest, like fiction; it was honest with *itself*, to its own rules, like a controlled experiment, a way to learn. It was a game, sort of. . . .

JUDGE: David! This is not a game.

DAVID: Well, then it's a gimmick; and that's worse because that's *dis*honest. It's like jazz masses and chancel dramas and flannel graphs and sewing circles and billiards in the church basement. It's the same old come-on in a bright new package. It's dishonest.

JUDGE: This is no game, gentlemen. And there's not much time. We will dispense with these usual opening speeches about the folly of our venture and get on with the task at hand.

DAVID [*trying hard to communicate and to control himself*]: But any real trial is over. Who's interested? As far as the college students are concerned Jesus is a dead issue. Sweet Jesus, gentle Jesus, good old Jesus fell asleep for them somewhere in their high school years. Let the dead. . . .

JOHN: David.

DAVID [*still to the* JUDGE]: Do you know what your friends are saying? You're a sick old man who isn't fit to be pastor. You've flipped. If Jesus Christ had any dignity among us, you've destroyed it with your stupid trial, your. . . .

JOHN: David don't! [*To the* JUDGE] Some of us do think that Jesus is still important. College students haven't all forgotten. But he's got a point, Pastor.

JUDGE: In this courtroom you will address me as "Your honor."

DAVID [*loses control altogether*]: Oh, this is hopeless. You don't listen—your honor—or understand or anything. Let's quit.

JUDGE: I understand, David. You made a commitment to try Jesus Christ before as many witnesses as possible. You made a commitment to partake in his proof, to help in proving him before a massed jury of skeptics, to present him before *people,* David. You made a commitment, once, to do that in every way possible. You made a commitment. And this trial is highly symbolical of that commitment. Oh, I understand. Now that the trial *is* coming to a close you don't want to face the consequences. You are afraid to. Search the symbolism in that, David. You try to understand. If your position—and your commitment—is worth anything, prove it before this court. Then, maybe, the people will listen to you. The students, too, David. Find yourself worthy here, and even the students will begin to turn to you again. Do you see? Do you understand what I'm trying to get across with this whole trial? David?

DAVID [*looking away*]: Summon the witnesses to Jesus' death and finish this thing. I'm sick of it.

JOHN [*after questioning the* JUDGE *with his eyes and receiving a slow nod*]: The defense calls the centurion to the stand.

JUDGE: Does the prosecution have any objection to calling this witness?

DAVID: He'll do.

JUDGE: Please take the stand. [*Rises from the congregation and comes forward.*] Do you swear to tell the truth, the whole truth, and nothing but the truth?

STEVE: I do.

JOHN: Steve, why did you take this part?

STEVE: I was in Viet Nam. I think I can put myself in the shoes of a military man, like the centurion.

JOHN: I hear you were distinguished for bravery on the battlefield. . . .

DAVID: Do we have to have all this . . . this personal history?

JOHN [*genuine*]: Sorry, David. Steve, have you seen many men die?

STEVE: Yes.

JOHN: Is there any difference in the way men die?

STEVE: Yes, sir.

JOHN: Could you describe some of the ways?

STEVE: Well, yes. Yes, sir, I could. Some men fight death; they're angry, but it's a private thing with them; they fight quietly, as if death were another man, as if it were a bitter, bitter wrestling match. You hear them breathe through their nose, but that's all. The fight is too important. Some men scream and scream with their tongues hanging out. . . .

DAVID [*quietly, almost preoccupied*]: Objection. [*Nobody notices and* STEVE *doesn't stop.*]

STEVE: . . . Scream things like, "Why?" or "Please" or "No"; look at their wet guts and scream "No." Some just turn over in the dirt and cry. Some talk, then they laugh, and then the blood spurts with every laugh. Some are calm. Some . . . a few [DAVID *senses something and looks up*] . . . say they are going to join God in heaven. And some try to make amends. . . .

DAVID [*says*]: Objection.

STEVE: . . . for their life by doing one good thing before they die. . . . You can learn a lot. . . .

DAVID [*indignant*]: Objection! Objection, your honor. This is all preliminary. This is Steve talking and not the Centurion. It's about Viet Nam and not about Gaul or Rome or Palestine or wherever they threw spears at each other. Yeah, it's about Napalm, *not* spears, and that has nothing to do with this trial.

JOHN: Oh, come on now, David. Dying hasn't changed over the years; both Steve and the Centurion know the same thing from experience. But I'll address him as "Centurion" if you really want to press the rules.

DAVID: I *do* want.

JOHN: Okay. Can you cite any occasion, Centurion, when the words of a dying man gave you special insight into his character?

STEVE: Yes, sir. Jim Baxter was. . . .

DAVID: NO sir! Jim Baxter has nothing to do with this trial! Steve knew him, but the Centurion did not; and Jim Baxter is nowhere in the Bible. Your honor, Steve swore to tell the truth. What is that? What is that truth? What he knows or what the Bible says? What the Bible says the *Centurion* knew? Okay, John, death hasn't changed over the years. But we have. I mean, we weren't there, and all we've got for evidence in this trial—to make this trial honest—is the Bible's word for it. According to every rule, *there's* the truth: in the Bible, not in Steve. And Jim Baxter is not in the Bible. No, sir. I object. To the line of questioning, to the proceedings, to the trial . . . the whole deal.

JUDGE [*he has been patient*]: Objection sustained. He's got a point, John. Steve is here as the Centurion; let him tell his soldier experience and memories only where they could be the Centurion's as well. Change your stories, Steve, to fit your role. As much as possible, stick to the truth.

JOHN: At this time, then, the defense would like to introduce as evidence one of the documents which record the testimony of the centurion at the time of Jesus' death. This testimony is in the report of the Gospel of Matthew, chapter 27.

JUDGE: Will the prosecution accept this document as evidence?

DAVID [*incredulous*]: Of course.

JOHN: According to the record, Matthew says that "when the centurion and those who were with him, keeping watch over Jesus, saw the earthquake and what took place, they were filled with awe, and said, 'Truly this was the Son of God.' " Is this a faithful report of what happened, Centurion?

STEVE: Yes, sir; it is.

JOHN: Good. Tell us what incidents connected with the death of Jesus led you and others at the crucifixion to make that statement?

STEVE: Well, first there was the earthquake. It was a sign to all of us that God was involved. He was endorsing the death of Jesus Christ as part of his own program of salvation.

DAVID [*calm and intellectual now; this is the way he wants it*]: Proves nothing; it's a separate incident and the centurion is interpreting.

JOHN [*a little tired of interference*]: This isn't a debate, David, it's a trial. Now *you* follow the rules. Besides, what about the three hours' darkness?

DAVID: Eclipse.

JUDGE: Gentlemen.

JOHN: I'm sorry, your honor. Centurion, is there anything in the record which would provide a clue to the character of Jesus at the time of death?

STEVE: Before they crucified him someone offered him wine mixed with gall, but he refused it.

JOHN: Ah, yes. What was the purpose of that drink?

STEVE: It was like a drug to kill the pain. Jesus refused so that he could suffer all of the pain for his followers. It was deliberate.

DAVID: I object. . . .

JUDGE: You object too much, young man. Overruled. Listen and prepare your own case.

JOHN: Your honor, we are searching to find out whether or not Jesus is the Son of God. There are several ways to discover what a man is. I want to investigate two of them: what he did and what he said at the time of his death. I've already begun the first. I would like to complete it and then go on to the second. Is the plan clear, David?

DAVID: The plan *was* clear, John. [*Without looking at* JOHN.]

JOHN [*waits, and then to* STEVE]: Go on.

STEVE: Well, after Jesus was crucified, people stood around the cross and ranked on him. They cut him with his own words, "If you are the Son of God, come down from the cross."

JOHN: Why do you suppose he didn't come down?

STEVE: Oh, he could have. But dying was part of the plan, you see. He announced that earlier to his disciples.

[*David registers exasperation at* STEVE's *testimony, but says nothing.*]

JOHN: Centurion, what did Jesus *do*?

STEVE: Nothing. That's the point. No miracle, no words during that whole scene. Nothing. He *could* have done anything; but that would have been the easy way. Any man would have done something. That's the difference with Jesus. It's hard for a man to keep still at anytime. Mock him and he's going to fight, or cry, or something. Crucify him, and you know he's going to get angry. But Jesus, with all the power he had, kept absolutely still. He did nothing. If you look at it right, *that's* the miracle. He had to be more than a man.

DAVID: A stiff.

JOHN: David!

DAVID: Sorry, sorry. I let my interpretation slip.

JOHN [*a sincere effort to reach* DAVID, *who is looking away—and has been for most of* STEVE's *testimony*]: Listen, David, we don't have to. . . . [*He thinks better of it; to* STEVE] Could we concentrate on what Jesus said just before he died. Your honor, I want to enter Luke's passion text as evidence along with the Matthew text.

JUDGE: If there are no objections. . . . It shall be recorded, then.

JOHN: Okay, Centurion, his words.

STEVE: Yes, sir. [*These "yes sir's" vary as* STEVE *is more or less sure of what is going on between* JOHN *and* DAVID; STEVE *is not stupid, but any mind quicker than his own bewilders him until it commands him; then he finds his tongue.*] Umm; soon after Jesus had been nailed up he said something that made an impression on me and some of the men. He said, "Father, forgive them. They don't know what they're doing." He expressed his love for his murderers, for all men.

JOHN: The report of Jesus' death in Matthew, does it give any of his words?

STEVE: Yes, sir; one saying.

JOHN: What is it?

STEVE: Jesus began to recite the twenty-second Psalm.

JOHN: How does it begin?

STEVE: My God, my God, why have you forsaken me?

JOHN: What other cries did you hear from Jesus' lips?

STEVE: We heard him talk to God. He whispered. They were his last words, "Into your hands I commend my spirit."

JOHN: Centurion, anything else?

STEVE: Oh, yes. Yes, sir. At one point he had a talk with one of the robbers hanging next to him. The robber admitted his guilt and asked Jesus to remember him when he became king. Then Jesus said, "Truly, I say to you, today you will be with me in Paradise."

JOHN: What do you think that meant?

STEVE [*delighted that his opinion is still of importance*]: Well, Jesus acquitted this man and announced his acceptance before God. There the robber would join Jesus in bliss. Jesus' saying here was another indication that he was the real king, the future king who could and would decide the fate of men. . . .

JOHN: In view of these actions and sayings of Jesus during his last hours, what is your conclusion about the character of Jesus?

STEVE: It is my conviction that Jesus is the Son of God.

JOHN: The defense rests, your honor.

DAVID: Well done, John. Simple, but moving. Moving. A strong emotional stance. . . .

JUDGE: Would you please proceed with the prosecution and keep your personal feelings to yourself?

DAVID [*with measured strength in every word*]: My

personal feelings? Your honor, I just heard a case *based* on personal feelings! Oh, but never mind. I think I'll say something to that later. We are among honorable men; the trial must be honorable.

JUDGE: Don't be impertinent, young man. There *is* a limit.

DAVID: Your honor, you sound like a pastor! [*The* JUDGE *is left in silence, and* DAVID *turns to* STEVE.] How many earthquakes have you felt, soldier?

STEVE: Four, I believe.

DAVID: And how many eclipses of the sun have you seen?

STEVE: Maybe three.

DAVID: And each time there was an eclipse, each time there was an earthquake, did you think God was giving you some special sign about the meaning of Jesus' death?

STEVE: No, but when Jesus died there was an earthquake and an eclipse. . . .

DAVID: How do you know the quake and eclipse weren't signs of something else, soldier? Signs for the two robbers, a quake for the bad, an eclipse for the good; or both quake and eclipse for the bad because God was so frightfully angry; or. . . .

STEVE: No sir; they were signs of God's approval.

DAVID: I see. God approves every death that coincides with an earthquake.

STEVE: No; this one was different.

DAVID: How, soldier?

STEVE: I don't know, but it was.

JOHN: David, this is unfair. How can Steve give any more details than we have in the documents?

DAVID: Then he shouldn't make unwarranted conclusions—not in the documents.

JOHN: You drove him to it.

DAVID: Oh, no. He believes it; he believes it! Let him
prove it. You were no help there. You were his
tender mother over his faith, but you were bliss-
fully ignorant about proofs. . . .

JUDGE: Gentlemen, this court will hold you both in
contempt. You are acting like little children who
won't keep to the rules.

DAVID [*whirling on the* JUDGE *and holding him in icy
contempt*]: Why, Pastor!

JUDGE [*continuing quietly and less sure of himself*]:
Go on with your examination.

DAVID: It seems, soldier, you have made a specialty
of hearing the last words of dying men. Is that so?

STEVE: I am a soldier; that's all.

DAVID: And do you think that the way men die on the
battlefield is somehow comparable to the way men
die on the cross?

STEVE: I don't see why not. They suffer the same way.

DAVID: You testified that some men scream violently
when they die. Is that right?

STEVE: Yes, sir.

DAVID: And you maintain that Jesus screamed the
words, "My God, My God, why have you forsaken
me . . . ?"

STEVE: I didn't say he screamed.

DAVID: Is there a difference, soldier?

STEVE: What do you mean?

DAVID: Dying men scream, "Why?" Jesus screams,
"Why?" Is there a difference, soldier? Jesus accuses
God of forsaking him, deserting him, leaving him

to die. Is there a difference between Jesus' scream and that of any other forsaken man?

STEVE: Jesus didn't accuse God. . . .

DAVID: God didn't come to help him, did he?

STEVE: No, but. . . .

DAVID: And he died forsaken?

STEVE: Yes, but that was part of the plan of God.

DAVID: Just answer the question, soldier. Forget your opinions for once. Did he die forsaken by God or not?

STEVE: Yes.

DAVID: The difference, soldier. Where's the difference?

STEVE: I don't. . . .

JOHN: Objection. I object.

DAVID: Shut up. You can't object. This is the first time we have anything like a proper trial.

JOHN: But. . . .

DAVID: Shut up, John! Soldier, what were Jesus' words about the future joys of the robber?

STEVE: Today you will be with me in Paradise.

DAVID: Let's look at this one a moment. Would you say Jesus was doing a good deed for the robber?

STEVE: In a way, yes.

DAVID: In just the same way that "some men try to make amends for their life by doing one good thing before they die?" You said it, soldier; those are your words.

STEVE: I know; but it's not the same with Jesus. It's more than that.

DAVID: How, soldier? How is it more? *Where is the difference,* soldier? What things in the record say

Jesus' action was more than a hero's last gesture?

STEVE: He asked God to forgive the murderers who nailed him to the cross.

DAVID: Neat. A way to soothe his guilty conscience before he died; another good deed; the words of a deluded dreamer. . . . There is no difference. Jesus' death was the same as any other death.

STEVE: Pastor, didn't you tell us the things I said were true? They are true aren't they?

DAVID: They are opinions, Steve, can't you see that? They are your personal conclusions. They are matters of faith, not matters of fact. And in a court of law they are absolutely worthless. Right, judge?

JUDGE: Well, I suppose. . . .

DAVID [*through this whole speech to the end* DAVID *rises to a climax, overrides and ignores every interruption. He will talk now*]: No jury could conclude that this Jesus of Nazareth was the Son of God. He loses. He cannot be what he said he was. He is guilty of the highest, the grossest, the most damnable deception. Even today, for all our progress, no honest court of law could find Jesus innocent. Courts are what they always were. The Sanhedrin wasn't wrong! Jesus was. And right now, according to every logical principle, I am not wrong; Jesus is. Now, your honor, the trial *is* over . . . [*pauses.*]

JUDGE: Then let us proceed with the concluding remarks of the defense.

DAVID [*ignoring the directives of the* JUDGE]: . . . not because your Lord is found guilty all over again. The trial is done because I quit. I'm sick of every institution, every organization, every person who handles Jesus Christ like a matter of fact. That's what happened in this trial. That's what is happening in the church. You grope about to prove that Jesus was the Son of God. Where's your proof? Where, Pastor? In your study? In your books? In your neat logic? In your sparkling sermons? In your endless meetings and musings? In your goddam trials?

JUDGE: That's enough, David.

DAVID: I'm not through yet. Look. Until Steve broke down just now he *was* proving that Jesus was something more than a man. And then he broke down under *your* system.

JOHN [*feeling the impact of* DAVID's *words*]: David! Haven't you gone far enough?

DAVID: Oh, yes, and then there's my commitment, my eternal, neon commitment. Sir, I suspended that commitment to follow the rules of your trial; and let me say that I alone followed those rules. Now I intend to take that commitment up again. I will shake hands with Steve because he is a man like me. Then I will leave this church of yours. This is no court. It cannot prove Jesus is God. But Jesus *as* God puts us on trial so as to acquit us. Judge, you are no judge. You haven't got the right. [*Crosses over to* STEVE *and leaves.*]

JUDGE: There were two of you, John. You were brothers and you weren't so very different from one another. Why did David never learn respect? [*John knows, but he can neither leave nor explain. So he sits down.*]

About the Authors

Richard Urdahl is University Pastor of Waterloo Lutheran University, Ontario. He was formerly a campus minister at Purdue University. The title play for this book is his first play to be published.

Walter Wangerin is a young poet, playwright, and actor who has studied at Concordia Seminary in Saint Louis. His poetry has appeared in a number of college magazines. He teaches English at the University of Evansville, Indiana.

George Churley is also a budding young playwright and actor. A recent graduate of Concordia Teacher's College in Seward, Nebraska, he hopes to work on a college or high school staff, creating new forms of dramatic communication.

Warren Kliewer is an established poet, playwright, director, and literary artist. He is professor of English, Speech, and Drama at Wichita State University in Kansas and coeditor of the journal *Religious Theatre*. His books include *Moralities and Miracles, The Violators,* and *Red Rose and Gray Cowl;* his plays include *Seventy Times Seven* and *A Trial Can Be Fun, If You're the Judge.*

James Stuckey served for some years as a professor of speech at McCormick Theological Seminary in Chicago. He is now Director for the Arts of Market Place Ministers in Alexandria, Virginia.

PB#1

ABOUT THE AUTHORS

William Urbrock now teaches religion at Lycoming College in Pennsylvania, having just completed his work in Old Testament at Harvard University.

Jerome Nilssen is well known. *The Drowning, the Dancing* and *Saturday Waiting* are recent works from his pen (published by Fortress Press). He is the author of many plays and is now professor of church and society at Hamma School of Theology in Springfield, Ohio.

Norman Habel is the consulting editor of the Fortress Press Open Books series and the author of *For Mature Adults Only* and *Interrobang,* two books in that series. He teaches Old Testament at Concordia Seminary in Saint Louis.